Crypto for Beginners: A Step-by-Step Guide to Digital Currency Investing and Trading

Comprehensive and Detailed Guide to Cryptocurrency Investing, Including Crypto ETFs and the Blockchain Industry

By Dr Israel Carlos Lomovasky

Copyright(C)Dr Israel Carlos Lomovasky 2024

About the Book

Discover the Ultimate Guide to Cryptocurrency Investing

Are you ready to dive into the exciting world of cryptocurrencies? "Crypto for Beginners: A Step-by-Step Guide to Digital Currency Investing" is your comprehensive, accessible, and essential resource for navigating the dynamic landscape of digital currencies. This book is meticulously designed to cater to both novices and those looking to deepen their understanding of cryptocurrency investing.

Why This Book Stands Out

Comprehensive Coverage:

- **Foundational Knowledge:** Understand the basics of cryptocurrencies, blockchain technology, and the principles driving this revolutionary market.
- **Advanced Topics:** Explore complex concepts like Decentralized Finance (DeFi), Non-Fungible Tokens (NFTs), staking, and yield farming, all explained in an easy-to-understand manner.
- **Crypto ETFs:** Get detailed insights into the newly available crypto ETFs, a crucial investment vehicle for diversifying your portfolio.

Accessible and User-Friendly:

- **Step-by-Step Guidance:** Detailed instructions and practical tips to help you get started with cryptocurrency investing, from setting up wallets to making your first trade.
- **Real-World Examples:** Illustrations and case studies using real-world data to provide a clear understanding of market trends and investment strategies.

Who Should Read This Book?

New Investors:

- If you are new to the world of cryptocurrencies and looking to understand the basics, this book provides a solid foundation to start your journey.

Experienced Investors:

- For those who are familiar with traditional investing but want to explore the cryptocurrency market, this guide offers advanced strategies and insights into integrating digital assets into your portfolio.

Tech Enthusiasts:

- Anyone interested in the technological advancements of blockchain and its applications will find valuable information about the future of finance and digital assets.

Finance Professionals:

- Professionals in the financial sector looking to stay updated with the latest trends and innovations in the crypto world will benefit from the detailed analysis and market insights provided.

What You Will Learn

Introduction to Cryptocurrencies:

- **History and Evolution:** From the birth of Bitcoin to the rise of altcoins, understand the historical context and future potential of digital currencies.
- **Blockchain Technology:** Learn about the underlying technology that powers cryptocurrencies, including its security and transparency features.

Investing Strategies:

- **Long-Term Holding vs. Active Trading:** Discover different investment strategies and choose the one that aligns with your financial goals and risk tolerance.
- **Portfolio Building:** Learn how to create a balanced and diversified cryptocurrency portfolio tailored to different risk levels.

Advanced Investment Vehicles:

- **Crypto ETFs:** Understand the benefits and risks of investing in Crypto ETFs and how to incorporate them into your investment strategy.
- **DeFi and NFTs:** Explore the innovative world of decentralized finance and non-fungible tokens, including how to invest in these emerging sectors.

Staying Safe and Informed:

- **Security Best Practices:** Protect your investments with robust security measures, including the use of secure wallets and two-factor authentication.
- **Market Analysis:** Stay updated with reliable news sources, participate in online communities, and continuously learn from industry experts.

Why You Need This Book

"Crypto for Beginners: A Step-by-Step Guide to Digital Currency Investing" is more than just a book; it's your gateway to the future of finance. Whether you are just starting out or looking to expand your investment knowledge, this guide will equip you with the tools and confidence needed to navigate the cryptocurrency market successfully.

Get your copy today and embark on a transformative journey into the world of digital currency investing!

Table of Contents

Introduction

1. **Welcome to the World of Cryptocurrencies**
    - Brief history and evolution of cryptocurrencies
    - The importance and relevance of digital currencies in today's financial landscape
    - What readers can expect to learn from this book

Chapter 1: Understanding Cryptocurrencies

1. **What Are Cryptocurrencies?**
   - Definition and basic concepts
   - Differences between cryptocurrencies and traditional currencies
2. **The Birth of Bitcoin**
   - Origins and creation by Satoshi Nakamoto
   - The technology behind Bitcoin
3. **Beyond Bitcoin: Other Popular Cryptocurrencies**
   - Overview of major cryptocurrencies (Ethereum, Ripple, Litecoin, etc.)
   - Key differences and unique features of each

Chapter 2: The Blockchain Technology

1. **What Is Blockchain?**
   - Explanation of blockchain technology
   - How it works and why it's secure
2. **Types of Blockchains**
   - Public vs. private blockchains
   - Examples and use cases
3. **Smart Contracts and Decentralized Applications (DApps)**
   - Definition and functionality
   - Real-world applications

Chapter 3: Setting Up for Success

1. **Choosing a Cryptocurrency Wallet**
   - Types of wallets (hot vs. cold)
   - How to set up and secure your wallet
2. **Understanding Cryptocurrency Exchanges**
   - Centralized vs. decentralized exchanges
   - How to choose the right exchange for you
3. **Regulations and Legal Considerations**
   - Overview of global cryptocurrency regulations
   - Legal issues and how to stay compliant

Chapter 4: Investing in Cryptocurrencies

1. **Investment Strategies**

- Long-term holding (HODLing) vs. active trading
- Diversification and risk management
2. **Analysing Cryptocurrencies**
    - Fundamental analysis
    - Technical analysis
    - Sentiment analysis
3. **Building Your Crypto Portfolio**
    - Steps to create a balanced portfolio
    - Example portfolios for different risk tolerances

Chapter 5: Trading Cryptocurrencies

1. **Introduction to Crypto Trading**
    - Basic trading concepts
    - Types of orders (market, limit, stop-loss)
2. **Technical Analysis Tools**
    - Chart patterns and indicators
    - Using tools like Moving Averages, RSI, MACD
3. **Developing a Trading Plan**
    - Setting goals and limits
    - Keeping track of your trades and performance

Chapter 6: Staying Informed and Safe

1. **Crypto News and Resources**
    - Reliable sources for cryptocurrency news
    - Community forums and educational resources
2. **Security Best Practices**
    - Protecting your investments from scams and hacks
    - Importance of two-factor authentication and regular updates
3. **Recognizing and Avoiding Scams**
    - Common cryptocurrency scams and how to spot them
    - Steps to take if you suspect fraudulent activity

Chapter 7: Crypto ETFs: A New Frontier

1. **Introduction to Crypto ETFs**
    - What are Crypto ETFs and how they work

- Benefits of investing in Crypto ETFs
2. **Types of Crypto ETFs**
    - Physically-backed ETFs
    - Futures-based ETFs
    - Equity-based ETFs (investing in blockchain-related companies)
3. **Popular Crypto ETFs**
    - Overview of leading ETFs such as ProShares Bitcoin Strategy ETF, Grayscale Bitcoin Trust, and others
4. **How to Invest in Crypto ETFs**
    - Steps to buying crypto ETFs through traditional brokerage accounts
    - Understanding fees and management costs
5. **Risks and Considerations**
    - Volatility and tracking errors
    - Regulatory risks and market sentiment

Chapter 8: Advanced Topics

1. **DeFi (Decentralized Finance)**
    - Overview of DeFi and its potential impact
    - Key DeFi platforms and how to invest in them
2. **NFTs (Non-Fungible Tokens)**
    - What are NFTs and how they work
    - Investing in NFTs: opportunities and risks
3. **Staking and Yield Farming**
    - How to earn passive income with cryptocurrencies
    - Platforms and strategies for staking and yield farming

Conclusion

1. **The Future of Cryptocurrencies**
    - Potential developments and trends in the crypto world
    - Final thoughts and encouragement for beginners
2. **Next Steps for New Investors**
    - Continuous learning and staying updated
    - Building a long-term investment strategy

Appendices

1. **Glossary of Cryptocurrency Terms**
    - Definitions of key terms and jargon
2. **Useful Tools and Resources**
    - List of recommended wallets, exchanges, and analysis tools
3. **Frequently Asked Questions (FAQ)**
    - Common questions and concise answers for beginners

This table of contents provides a comprehensive and detailed guide for beginners in cryptocurrency investing, including a dedicated chapter on the newly available crypto ETFs, ensuring readers are well-informed about this emerging investment vehicle.

DISCLAIMER
The material provided in this book is for informational and educational purposes only and is not intended to be taken as trading or investing advice. The content provided is intended to help you better understand various trading and investing strategies and techniques, but it is not a substitute for professional advice. You should always consult with a licensed financial advisor before making any investment decisions. Additionally, trading and investing in securities involves risk, and you should never invest money that you cannot afford to lose. It is your responsibility to comply with all relevant laws and regulations, including those related to securities trading, in your jurisdiction. By using this book, you agree to hold

harmless the author and the publisher from any liability arising out of your use of the information provided.
Any investment decisions made by the user through the use of such content is solely based on the user's independent analysis taking into
consideration your financial circumstances, investment objectives and risk
tolerance found therein unless specifically authorized to do so.
The author is not registered as a securities broker-dealer or an investment
adviser either with the U.S. Securities and Exchange Commission (the
"SEC") or with any state or overseas securities regulatory authority.The Author is not licensed to provide investment advice.

About the author

Curriculum Vitae

Education:

- Doctor of Science (DSc) in Project Evaluation, Technion, Haifa, Israel
- Master of Science (MSc) in Operations Research, London School of Economics
- Bachelor of Science (BSc) in Industrial and Management Engineering, Technion, Haifa, Israel

Teaching and Academic Research Positions Held:

- Micro Economics
- Macro Economics
- Econometrics

- Statistics
- Mathematics
- Public Finance
- Urban Planning Mathematical Models
- Transportation Science

Urban and Regional Planning Experience:

- Comprehensive Urban Renewal Project Manager (Physical and Social Project) of the East Acco Government Project. Received the title Yakir Acco from the Acco municipality.

Professional Experience:

- Founding partner (2006-2011) in the company "Kaul and Lomovasky Holdings Inc" specializing in the computerization of trading using artificial intelligence.
- Internet and Artificial Intelligence Programmer, Developer, and Consultant (2012-2018).
- Developed an AI-based system to calculate the price of apartments in 300 towns in Israel, using VBA Excel Neural Networks (artificial intelligence) pre-processing and presented the prices on a Python Django-based website.
- (2018-2024)Author of several books on topics such as algorithmic trading, quantum computing, crypto trading, artificial intelligence, and startup ideas.

Computer Programming Skills:

- C, VBA under Excel, Microsoft Office, HTML, PHP, MATLAB, SAS, Python, Django, Keras, Panda, Cloud AI Applications, TensorFlow, Google Cloud Platform, OpenCV, Adversarial GANs, Computer Vision, Image Classification, Object Recognition, Pose Recognition.
- Quantum computing and quantum machine learning.
- Algorithm development, end-to-end ownership.

Publications

-Quantum Wealth: Mastering Investments in the Quantum Computing Boom.: Quantum Opportunities: Investing in Breakthrough Technologies. Foundations to Advanced. Kindle Edition
by Dr Israel Carlos Lomovasky (Author) Format: Kindle Edition

-AI Investment Mastery: How to Outperform the Market with AI Assets: Comprehensive. Investing in AI Stocks, ETFs, Mutual Funds, Venture Capital, Private ... Foundations to Advanced (FINANCE Book 9) Kindle Edition
by Dr Israel Carlos Lomovasky (Author) Format: Kindle Edition

Book 8 of 8: FINANCE

-The Quantum Nexus: AI, Blockchain, and the Future of Everything: How these Cutting-edge Technologies will Converge to Reshape Various Industries and Everyday ... - Futurology - Science fiction Book 8) Kindle Edition
by Dr Israel Carlos Lomovasky (Author) Format: Kindle Edition

Book 7 of 7: Future sciences - Futurology - Science fiction

-Coding the Citizen's Voice: Python Tools for MOTMSDD in Governance and Planning: the Manual: Python Source Code. AI & Data Science. Metaverse of the Minds ... and Brain Computer Interface Book 9) Kindle Edition
by Dr Israel Carlos Lomovasky (Author) Format: Kindle Edition

Book 8 of 8: The future implications of the combination between the Internet, the Metaverse and Brain Computer Interface

-Beyond the Vote: AI Applications in Direct Democracy and Civic Engagement: Integrating AI, ML, NLP, Data Visualization, and MOTMSDD Into Public Governance ... and Brain Computer Interface Book 8) Kindle Edition
by Dr Israel Carlos Lomovasky (Author) Format: Kindle Edition

Beyond Quantum: The Next Leap in Computational Paradigms: Exploring the Future of Advanced Computing Technologies (Quantum Computing Book 5) Kindle Edition
by Dr Israel Carlos Lomovasky (Author) Format: Kindle Edition

Book 5 of 5: Quantum Computing

-AI-Proof Your Career: Building Resilience in the Face of Automation: Strategies for Healthcare,Finance,Manufacturing,Art,Entertainment,Retail, Transportation,Energy,Logistics,Government,Teaching Kindle Edition
by Dr Israel Carlos Lomovasky (Author) Format: Kindle Edition

-Defensive Trading in Crypto ETFs: Protecting Your Portfolio in Volatile Markets: The Damage and Losses Control Bible for The Crypto ETFs Investor and Trader Kindle Edition
by Dr Israel Carlos Lomovasky (Author) Format: Kindle Edition

Book 11 of 11: TRADING

-Algorithmic Trading for Everyone: A Non-Programmer's Journey to Automation: Comprehensive Introduction to Algo Trading for Beginners Without Programming Background Kindle Edition
by Dr Israel Carlos Lomovasky (Author) Format: Kindle Edition

Book 10 of 10: TRADING

-The Great Crypto Illusion: Navigating the Future of Valueless Assets : Examining the Sustainability of Cryptocurrencies Without Traditional Intrinsic Value. (FINANCE Book 8) Kindle Edition
by Dr Israel Carlos Lomovasky (Author) Format: Kindle Edition

-Navigating Crypto ETFs Trading: An Absolute Beginners Guide to New Markets: Foundations of Crypto ETF Trading: Building Your Digital Investment Portfolio Kindle Edition
by Dr Israel Carlos Lomovasky (Author) Format: Kindle Edition

-Profit and Protect: Retail Trading Strategies to Manage Risk and Grow Your Wealth: Foundations to Advanced. Stocks, Bonds, Crypto, Commodities & Forex. Hedging with Options, Swaps, Futures & More Kindle Edition
by Dr Israel Carlos Lomovasky (Author) Format: Kindle Edition

-The Future Game: Unleashing AI and Quantum Computing Power in Game Theory.: Beginners to Advanced.Python Code.Case studies:Economics,Finance,Politics,Environment,Social Science,Psychology,Health,More Kindle Edition
By Dr Israel Carlos Lomovasky (Author) Format: Kindle Edition

-AI and Quantum Strategies: Python's Role in Economic Innovation: Foundations to Advanced. With python and Quantum Code in a Computational Economics Range of Case Studies Kindle Edition
by Dr Israel Carlos Lomovasky (Author) Format: **Kindle Edition**

-Quantum Computing in Finance: Bridging Theory and Practice with Python: Case Studies: Algorithmic Trading, Risk Management, Fraud Detection, Options Pricing ,Economic Forecasting and more
by Dr Israel Carlos Lomovasky (Author)

Book 6 of 6: FINANCE

-Artificial Gods: The Onset of Superior Machine Intelligence and Consciousness: : The Why and How of a Ban on Research Leading To Superintelligence And AI Consciousness Kindle Edition
by Dr Israel Carlos Lomovasky (Author)

-Quantum and Consciousness: Exploring the Mind-Computer Interface: Unveiling the Quantum Mind: Quantum Computing and the Fabric of Consciousness Kindle Edition
by Dr Israel Carlos Lomovasky (Author)

-Quantum Democracy: Unleashing MOTMSDD with Quantum Computing: MOTMSDD : Metaverse Of The Minds Social Direct Democracy (The future implications of the ... and Brain Computer Interface Book 6) Kindle Edition
by Dr Israel Carlos Lomovasky (Author)

-MOTMSDD: Metaverse Of The Minds Social Direct Democracy: Governance and Public Decision Making in The Era of Brain Computer Interface, AI and Metaverse, ... and Brain Computer Interface Book 5) Kindle Edition
by Dr Israel Carlos Lomovasky (Author)

-MOTMSDD Urbanism:Redefining Cities through AI and Metaverse of the Minds Social Direct Democracy: Sustainable Urbanism in the Age of Brain-Computer Interface.Solving Conflicts between Citizen's Needs Kindle Edition
by Dr Israel Carlos Lomovasky (Author)

-AI in Financial Markets: A Guide to Algorithmic Trading with ChatGPT: Python Code. CHATGPT Assistance. Basics to Advanced. Traditional and AI/ML Trading. (FINANCE Book 6) Kindle Edition
by Dr Israel Carlos Lomovasky (Author)

-Python for Financial Freedom: Algorithmic Strategies for Personal Wealth: Trading and Investing. Foundations to Advanced. AI/ML, Risk ,Tax ,and Money Management. Stocks & Crypto (FINANCE Book 5) Kindle Edition
by Dr Israel Carlos Lomovasky (Author)

-Quantum Foundations of Computer Vision: A Guide for Researchers and Practitioners: Python and Quantum Language Code. Future Proof Computer Vision (Quantum Computing Book 3) Kindle Edition
by Dr Israel Carlos Lomovasky (Author)

-MOTMSDD ECONOMICS: From Classical Economics, to Metaverse Of The Minds Social Direct Democracy Economics.: For The Next WELFARE ECONOMICS: Harnessing BCI ... the Metaverse . (FUTURE ECONOMICS Book 1) Kindle Edition
by Dr Israel Carlos Lomovasky (Author)

-Quantum Hedge: Unlocking the Future of Algorithmic Trading. : Python and Quantum Languages Code. Basics to Advanced. Stocks, Forex and Crypto. Theory and Hands on Practice. Kindle Edition
by Dr Israel Carlos Lomovasky (Author)

-Quantum Economics: Rethinking Macro and Micro in the Age of Quantum Computing: Theory and Practice: Python and Quantum Language Code Explained Step by Step (FUTURE ECONOMICS Book 2) Kindle Edition
by Dr Israel Carlos Lomovasky (Author)

-Driving with the Mind: Exploring MOTMSDD and Its Impact on Smart Cities and Autonomous Mobility: MOTMSDD: Metaverse of The Minds Social Direct Democracy: ... Meets The Metaverse (URBANISM Book 4) Kindle Edition
by Dr Israel Carlos Lomovasky (Author)

-AI in Fundamental Analysis: Uncovering Hidden Algorithmic Investment Opportunities with Python.: Machine,Reinforcement and Deep Learning.Complete AI-Driven ... Advanced.Risk Management. (FINANCE Book 2) Kindle Edition
by Dr Israel Carlos Lomovasky (Author)

-Python for AI and Creativity: Unleashing the Power of Artificial Intelligence in the Arts: Basics to Advanced.Visual Arts,Design,Music,Poetry,Storytelling, ... learning-Python Book 3) Kindle Edition
by Dr Israel Carlos Lomovasky (Author)

-Python for Machine Learning. From Intermediate to Advanced Guide With Code.: Unleash the Potential of Advanced Machine Learning in Python. Covering Many ... learning-Python Book 2) Kindle Edition
by Dr Israel Carlos Lomovasky (Author)

-Python for Smart Cities: Machine Learning and Artificial Intelligence Applications for Urban Planning and Infrastructure: Python in Action: ML/AI for Smart ... Infrastructure Management (URBANISM Book 2) Kindle Edition
by Dr Israel Carlos Lomovasky (Author)

-Python for Machine Learning: A Beginner's Guide.From Scratch to intermediate.: Basis For Algorithmic Finance, Trading, Healthcare, Industry, Transportation, ... learning-Python Book 1) Kindle Edition
by Dr Israel Carlos Lomovasky (Author)

-SINGULARITY'S VEIL: THE RISE AND FALL OF HUMANITY. : A TALE BETWEEN SCIENCE FICTION AND FUTUROLOGY. STOP ARTIFICIAL GENERAL INTELLIGENCE NOW. (Future sciences - Futurology - Science fiction Book 6) Kindle Edition
by Dr Israel Carlos Lomovasky (Author)

-KILLING THE BEAST. THE THREAT OF ADVANCING ARTIFICIAL GENERAL INTELLIGENCE.: A CALL TO BAN AGI.SURVIVAL OF HUMANITY ON THE LINE. A CONTRARIAN NARRATIVE ... - Futurology - Science fiction Book 5) Kindle Edition
by Dr Israel Carlos Lomovasky (Author)

-Day Trading Basics to Advanced:A Comprehensive Guide.From Scalping to AI/ML.Algorithmic Trading.Python Code.: Day Trading Decoded:Unlocking Secrets to Profitable Trading.Stocks,Crypto,Options,Forex Kindle Edition
by Dr Israel Carlos Lomovasky (Author)

-BEGINNER'S MACHINE LEARNING AND ARTIFICIAL INTELLIGENCE IN PYTHON FOR FINANCE: A GUIDE.: EXPLORING THE INTERSECTION OF FINANCE AND ML/AI: A PYTHON PRIMER Kindle Edition
by Dr Israel Carlos Lomovasky (Author)

-The Internet Of Minds (IOM). An Essay: The Future Implications of Brain Computer Interface
by Dr Israel Carlos Lomovasky (Author)

-CRYPTO TRADING TECHNICAL ANALYSIS: Apply the technical analysis indicators, time-frames and approaches that fit Crypto Currencies trading characteristics. Kindle Edition
by Dr Israel Carlos Lomovasky (Author)

-QUANTUM MACHINE LEARNING: A COMPREHENSIVE GUIDE WITH PRACTICAL EXAMPLES AND QUANTUM LANGUAGE IMPLEMENTATION: FROM BASICS TO ADVANCED.INCLUDES PYTHON CODE. (Quantum Computing Book 2) Kindle Edition
by Dr Israel Carlos Lomovasky (Author)

-CRYPTO BASICS TO ADVANCED. MAKE MONEY WITH CRYPTO.THE CRYPTO BUSINESS STARTUP BIBLE.: Investing ,trading and beyond. 20 Cryptocurrency profitable strategies. Over 100 startup ideas. Kindle Edition
by Dr Israel Carlos Lomovasky (Author)

-QUANTUM COMPUTING AND OPERATIONS RESEARCH.AN ESSAY.WHAT IS QC AND WHY IT MATTERS TO OR PRACTITIONERS.: THE FUTURE IMPLICATIONS OF QUANTUM COMPUTING ON OPTIMIZATION AND OPERATIONS RESEARCH. Kindle Edition
by Dr Israel Carlos Lomovasky (Author)

-ALGORITHMIC TRADING FROM SCRATCH TO AI/ML STRATEGIES IMPLEMENTED IN PYTHON.FOR CRYPTO,STOCKS,FOREX AND MORE.: RETAIL TRADING SYSTEMS FROM BASIC TO SOPHISTICATED STEP BY STEP. PYTHON FOR YOUR PROJECTS. Paperback – May 17, 2023
by Dr Israel Carlos Lomovasky (Author)

-CRYPTO SENTIMENT ALGO TRADING.PYTHON AND PSEUDO-CODE.: Algo Cryptocurrencies Trade: day, trend, news, swing, arbitrage, bots, contrarian, volume, event, seasonal ,and more strategies. Kindle Edition
by Dr Israel Carlos Lomovasky (Author)

-ALGORITHMIC TRADING STRATEGIES AND TECHNIQUES IN PYTHON, PSEUDO-CODE AND TRADESTATION CODE.: Get your projects started.20 most used techniques and strategies covering all tradeable assets. Kindle Edition
by Dr Israel Carlos Lomovasky (Author)
-ALGORITHMIC TRADING STRATEGIES AND TECHNIQUES IN PYTHON, PSEUDO-CODE AND TRADESTATION CODE.: Get your projects started.20 most used techniques and strategies covering all tradeable assets. Kindle Edition
by Dr Israel Carlos Lomovasky (Author)

-

Introduction

Section 1: Welcome to the World of Cryptocurrencies

1.1 Brief History and Evolution of Cryptocurrencies

The Birth of Bitcoin:

- **Creation by Satoshi Nakamoto in 2009:**
    - The journey of cryptocurrencies began with the enigmatic figure or group known as Satoshi Nakamoto. In October 2008, Nakamoto published the seminal white paper titled "Bitcoin: A Peer-to-Peer Electronic Cash System". This document laid the groundwork for Bitcoin, proposing a decentralized

digital currency that would enable direct transactions without the need for a central authority.
- On January 3, 2009, Nakamoto mined the first block of the Bitcoin blockchain, known as the Genesis Block. This block contained the message, "The Times 03/Jan/2009 Chancellor on brink of second bailout for banks," highlighting the motivation to create a financial system independent of traditional banks and governmental control.
- **Initial Use Case as a Decentralized Digital Currency:**
  - Bitcoin was designed as a form of digital cash, enabling peer-to-peer transactions that are secure, verifiable, and free from the control of any central authority. Early adopters saw Bitcoin as a revolutionary tool for financial freedom and privacy.
- **Key Milestones in Bitcoin's History:**
  - **First Transaction:** The first known Bitcoin transaction occurred on January 12, 2009, when Satoshi Nakamoto sent 10 bitcoins to Hal Finney, a computer scientist and early Bitcoin supporter.
  - **Major Price Surges:** Bitcoin's price has seen dramatic increases over the years. Notable surges include reaching $1,000 in November 2013, surpassing $20,000 in December 2017, and hitting an all-time high of over $60,000 in 2021. By now the Bitcoin is near the 72000.00 USD (June 2024)

Emergence of Altcoins:

- **Introduction of Other Cryptocurrencies:**
  - Following Bitcoin's success, many alternative cryptocurrencies, or "altcoins," were developed to improve upon Bitcoin or to serve different purposes. Litecoin, created by Charlie Lee in 2011, was designed to process transactions more quickly and with a different hashing algorithm (Scrypt).
  - Ethereum, introduced by Vitalik Buterin in 2015, expanded the potential of blockchain technology with the introduction of smart contracts—self-executing

contracts where the terms are directly written into code. This innovation paved the way for decentralized applications (DApps).
- **Unique Features and Innovations:**
  - **Ethereum:** Offers a versatile platform for decentralized applications, making it the second-largest cryptocurrency by market capitalization.
  - **Ripple (XRP):** Focuses on facilitating real-time, cross-border payments with minimal transaction fees.
  - **Initial Coin Offerings (ICOs):** These have become a popular method for new projects to raise funds by issuing their own tokens. Ethereum itself was funded through an ICO, raising over $18 million in 2014.

Growth of the Cryptocurrency Ecosystem:

- **Development of Cryptocurrency Exchanges and Wallets:**
  - The rise of platforms like Coinbase, Binance, and Kraken has made buying, selling, and storing cryptocurrencies more accessible to the general public. These exchanges offer a wide range of services, from simple trading interfaces to advanced features for seasoned investors.
  - Wallets, both hardware (like Ledger and Trezor) and software (like Trust Wallet and MetaMask), provide secure ways to store and manage digital assets.
- **The Rise of Decentralized Finance (DeFi) and Non-Fungible Tokens (NFTs):**
  - **DeFi:** Aims to recreate traditional financial systems such as loans and insurance using blockchain technology, reducing the need for intermediaries and increasing accessibility.
  - **NFTs:** Unique digital assets representing ownership of specific items like art, music, and virtual real estate. The NFT market exploded in 2021, with digital artworks selling for millions of dollars.
- **Increasing Institutional Adoption and Regulatory Developments:**

- Companies like Tesla and MicroStrategy have invested heavily in Bitcoin, signaling growing institutional interest. Financial services companies like PayPal and Visa have also begun integrating cryptocurrency services.
- Regulatory bodies are increasingly focusing on cryptocurrencies, aiming to balance innovation with consumer protection. In the U.S., the SEC and CFTC are actively involved in regulating the market, while the EU has proposed the Markets in Crypto-Assets (MiCA) framework.

1.2 The Importance and Relevance of Digital Currencies in Today's Financial Landscape

Decentralization and Financial Inclusion:

- **Providing Financial Services to the Unbanked and Underbanked:**
    - Cryptocurrencies offer financial services to individuals without access to traditional banking systems. For example, in countries like Venezuela and Zimbabwe, where hyperinflation has devalued local currencies, Bitcoin provides a stable alternative.
    - **Case Studies:** In Kenya, M-Pesa, a mobile payment system, has integrated Bitcoin, allowing users to send and receive money more efficiently.

Digital Gold:

- **Bitcoin's Role as a Store of Value and Hedge Against Inflation:**
    - Bitcoin is often compared to gold due to its limited supply and its function as a hedge against inflation. As central banks print more money, many investors turn to Bitcoin to preserve their wealth.

- o **Comparisons with Traditional Assets:** Unlike gold, Bitcoin is easily transferable and divisible, making it a more versatile store of value in the digital age.

Technological Innovation:

- **Impact of Blockchain Technology Beyond Finance:**
  - o Blockchain technology has applications far beyond cryptocurrencies. In supply chain management, companies like IBM's Food Trust use blockchain to enhance transparency and traceability from farm to table.
  - o **Examples in Various Industries:**
    - **Healthcare:** Blockchain is used to secure patient records and ensure privacy.
    - **Real Estate:** Property transactions are recorded on blockchains to reduce fraud and increase efficiency.

Economic and Social Impact:

- **Promoting Economic Freedom and Reducing Reliance on Traditional Financial Institutions:**
  - o Cryptocurrencies enable peer-to-peer transactions, reducing the need for intermediaries and increasing financial autonomy. This is particularly important in regions with unstable financial systems.
  - o **Reducing Transaction Costs and Enhancing Cross-Border Payments:**
    - Cryptocurrencies offer a cost-effective alternative for international remittances, which can be expensive and slow through traditional banking systems. Projects like Stellar aim to facilitate cross-border payments with minimal fees.

1.3 What Readers Can Expect to Learn from This Book

Foundational Knowledge:

- **Basic Concepts and Terminology:**
    - The book will cover essential terms such as blockchain, mining, wallets, and smart contracts, ensuring readers have a solid foundation to build upon.
- **Understanding the Underlying Technology:**
    - Detailed explanations of how blockchain works, the importance of cryptographic security, and the consensus mechanisms that maintain network integrity.

Practical Investing Guidance:

- **Setting Up and Securing a Cryptocurrency Wallet:**
    - Step-by-step instructions on choosing and setting up different types of wallets, from mobile and desktop to hardware wallets, with tips on securing them.
- **Choosing and Using Cryptocurrency Exchanges Safely:**
    - Guidance on selecting reputable exchanges, completing account verification, and executing trades safely.
- **Investment Strategies:**
    - Exploration of various investment approaches, including long-term holding (HODLing), dollar-cost averaging, and active trading.

Advanced Topics:

- **Introduction to DeFi and Its Opportunities:**
    - Insights into DeFi platforms, how they operate, and how to participate in decentralized lending, borrowing, and yield farming.
- **Understanding and Investing in NFTs:**
    - Explanation of what NFTs are, their use cases, and strategies for investing in digital art and collectibles.
- **Exploring New Investment Vehicles like Crypto ETFs:**

- Overview of newly available crypto ETFs, their benefits, and how they can be integrated into an investment portfolio.

Staying Safe and Informed:

- **Best Practices for Securing Digital Assets:**
  - Tips on protecting your investments from scams and hacks, including the use of two-factor authentication and regular updates.
- **Staying Updated with the Latest Developments:**
  - Resources for keeping up with news, market trends, and technological advancements in the cryptocurrency space.
- **Recognizing and Avoiding Common Scams:**
  - Identification of common scams and fraudulent schemes in the cryptocurrency world, and strategies to avoid them.

By the end of this book, readers will be equipped with the knowledge and tools needed to confidently navigate the world of cryptocurrency investing, from the basics of setting up a wallet to the complexities of decentralized finance and crypto ETFs.

This expanded introduction blueprint provides a comprehensive overview of the topics that will be covered in the book, setting the stage for a thorough exploration of cryptocurrency investing for beginners.

Chapter 1: What Are Cryptocurrencies?

Section 1: Definition and Basic Concepts

1.1 Definition of Cryptocurrencies

Explanation of Digital or Virtual Currencies:

Cryptocurrencies are digital or virtual currencies that leverage cryptography for security. Unlike traditional currencies issued by governments (fiat money), cryptocurrencies operate independently of a central authority, utilizing decentralized networks based on blockchain technology. The concept of a digital currency is not new, but cryptocurrencies distinguish themselves by their decentralized nature, which enhances security and transparency.

Decentralized Nature and Use of Cryptographic Techniques for Security:

Cryptocurrencies rely on cryptographic techniques to secure transactions, control the creation of additional units, and verify the transfer of assets. Cryptography ensures that transactions are secure and immutable, meaning once a transaction is recorded on the blockchain, it cannot be altered. This immutability is a key feature that helps prevent fraud and double-spending.

Examples of Cryptocurrencies:

- **Bitcoin (BTC):** The first and most well-known cryptocurrency, created by the pseudonymous Satoshi Nakamoto in 2009. Bitcoin introduced the concept of a decentralized digital currency and remains the most valuable and widely recognized cryptocurrency.
- **Ethereum (ETH):** Launched in 2015 by Vitalik Buterin, Ethereum introduced the concept of smart contracts—self-executing contracts with the terms directly written into code. This innovation has enabled the development of decentralized applications (DApps) on its platform.
- **Ripple (XRP):** Designed for facilitating real-time, cross-border payments with low transaction fees, Ripple has established partnerships with numerous financial institutions.

Key Characteristics of Cryptocurrencies:

Decentralization: Cryptocurrencies operate on decentralized networks, meaning no single entity has control over the entire network. This is achieved through distributed ledger technology, where copies of the ledger are maintained across multiple nodes (computers) around the world. This decentralization reduces the risk of a single point of failure and increases the resilience of the network.

Transparency: All transactions on a cryptocurrency network are recorded on a public ledger known as the blockchain. This ledger is accessible to anyone, providing transparency and the ability to verify transactions independently. Blockchain technology ensures that all participants can agree on the state of the ledger without needing a central authority.

Immutability: Once a transaction is recorded on the blockchain, it cannot be altered or deleted. This immutability is achieved through cryptographic hashing and consensus mechanisms that validate transactions before they are added to the blockchain. This feature ensures the integrity of the data and prevents tampering.

Anonymity/Pseudonymity: While cryptocurrency transactions are transparent and traceable, the identities of the users involved are not directly revealed. Instead, users operate under pseudonyms, which are typically their wallet addresses. This provides a level of privacy, although sophisticated analysis can sometimes link transactions to individuals.

1.2 Differences Between Cryptocurrencies and Traditional Currencies

Centralization vs. Decentralization:

- **Traditional Currencies (Fiat):** Fiat currencies, such as the US dollar, euro, and yen, are issued and regulated by central banks and governments. These authorities control the money

supply, set interest rates, and implement monetary policies to manage economic stability.
- **Cryptocurrencies:** Cryptocurrencies operate on decentralized networks without a central authority. The control and validation of transactions are distributed across a network of nodes, enhancing security and reducing the risk of centralized failures.

Physical vs. Digital:

- **Fiat Currencies:** Fiat currencies exist in both physical form (cash) and digital records (bank accounts, electronic transfers). Physical cash is tangible and can be used for in-person transactions.
- **Cryptocurrencies:** Cryptocurrencies exist solely in digital form. They are stored in digital wallets and transferred electronically. This digital nature allows for seamless global transactions without the need for physical presence or intermediaries.

Inflation Control:

- **Fiat Currencies:** Central banks control the supply of fiat money through monetary policies, such as adjusting interest rates and printing money. This control can lead to inflation if the money supply increases too rapidly.
- **Cryptocurrencies:** Many cryptocurrencies have a fixed supply. For example, Bitcoin's total supply is capped at 21 million coins, which prevents inflation caused by overproduction. The controlled supply helps maintain the value of the currency over time.

Transaction Processes:

- **Traditional Banking:** Traditional banking transactions often require intermediaries such as banks and payment processors. These intermediaries verify and process transactions, which can be slow and costly, especially for cross-border transfers.

- **Cryptocurrencies:** Cryptocurrency transactions are peer-to-peer, meaning they are conducted directly between users without intermediaries. This process is often faster and cheaper than traditional banking, making cryptocurrencies an attractive option for international payments and remittances.

This comprehensive overview provides a solid foundation for understanding what cryptocurrencies are, how they function, and how they differ from traditional currencies. It sets the stage for deeper exploration into the world of digital assets and blockchain technology.

Section 2: The Birth of Bitcoin

2.1 Origins and Creation by Satoshi Nakamoto

Satoshi Nakamoto:

- **The Pseudonymous Creator(s) of Bitcoin:**
    - Satoshi Nakamoto is the name used by the unknown person or group of people who developed Bitcoin. Despite numerous investigations and speculations, the true identity of Nakamoto remains a mystery. This anonymity has contributed to Bitcoin's decentralized ethos and mystique.
- **Release of the Bitcoin White Paper in 2008:**
    - On October 31, 2008, Nakamoto published the white paper titled "Bitcoin: A Peer-to-Peer Electronic Cash System." This nine-page document outlined the principles of a decentralized digital currency that would allow secure peer-to-peer transactions without relying on third-party intermediaries like banks. The white paper proposed a solution to the double-spending problem, a major issue in previous digital currency systems.

Genesis Block:

- **The First Block Mined on the Bitcoin Blockchain in January 2009:**
  - On January 3, 2009, Nakamoto mined the first block of the Bitcoin blockchain, known as the Genesis Block or Block 0. This block has a unique place in the Bitcoin blockchain as it was the foundation upon which the rest of the network was built.
- **The Significance of the Embedded Message:**
  - The Genesis Block contains the text "The Times 03/Jan/2009 Chancellor on brink of second bailout for banks." This message is widely interpreted as a commentary on the instability of the traditional banking system and the need for an alternative financial system. It reflects the context of the 2008 financial crisis and highlights Bitcoin's foundational philosophy of decentralization and financial independence.

2.2 The Technology Behind Bitcoin

Blockchain Technology:

- **Description of Blockchain as a Distributed Ledger:**
  - A blockchain is a decentralized digital ledger that records transactions across many computers in such a way that the registered transactions cannot be altered retroactively. This ensures transparency and security without the need for a central authority.
- **How Blocks Are Linked Together with Cryptographic Hashes:**
  - Each block in the blockchain contains a list of transactions. Blocks are linked together through cryptographic hashes. Each block has a unique hash and contains the hash of the previous block, forming a chain. This structure ensures the integrity of the blockchain, as altering any block would require altering all subsequent blocks.

Mining and Consensus Mechanism:

- **Explanation of Proof-of-Work (PoW):**
    - Bitcoin uses a Proof-of-Work (PoW) consensus mechanism. In PoW, miners compete to solve complex mathematical problems using computational power. The first miner to solve the problem gets to add a new block to the blockchain and is rewarded with newly created bitcoins (block reward) and transaction fees from the transactions included in the block.
- **Role of Miners in Validating Transactions and Securing the Network:**
    - Miners play a crucial role in the Bitcoin network by validating transactions and securing the network against attacks. They verify the authenticity of transactions and ensure that no double-spending occurs.
- **Reward System for Miners:**
    - Miners are incentivized through block rewards and transaction fees. Initially, the block reward was 50 bitcoins, but this reward halves approximately every four years (known as the halving). As of now, the block reward is 6.25 bitcoins. This reward system helps regulate the creation of new bitcoins and controls inflation.

Bitcoin Transactions:

- **How Transactions Are Processed and Recorded on the Blockchain:**
    - A Bitcoin transaction involves transferring bitcoins from one wallet to another. Each transaction is signed with a private key and then broadcasted to the network, where it is verified by miners. Once verified, the transaction is included in a block and added to the blockchain.
- **Importance of Private and Public Keys in Securing Transactions:**

- Bitcoin transactions are secured using cryptographic keys. The public key serves as an address to receive bitcoins, while the private key allows the owner to spend or transfer those bitcoins. It is crucial to keep the private key secure, as anyone with access to it can control the associated bitcoins.

This detailed section provides a comprehensive understanding of the origins and technology behind Bitcoin, setting the stage for readers to grasp the fundamental concepts of cryptocurrencies.

Chapter 2: The Blockchain Technology

Section 1: What Is Blockchain?

1.1 Explanation of Blockchain Technology

Definition:

- **Blockchain as a Distributed Ledger Technology:**
    - Blockchain is a type of distributed ledger technology (DLT) that records transactions across many computers in a network so that the record cannot be altered retroactively. This decentralized approach ensures that no single entity has control over the entire database, enhancing security and transparency.
    - The primary purpose of blockchain is to provide a secure and immutable record of transactions, ensuring data integrity and trust without the need for a central authority.

Key Components:

- **Blocks:**
    - Blocks are units of data that store information about transactions. Each block contains a list of

transactions, a timestamp, and a cryptographic hash of the previous block.
    - In addition to transaction data, blocks also include a nonce, a random number used to vary the output of the hash function and make the mining process secure and challenging.
- **Chain:**
    - The chain is formed by linking blocks together using cryptographic hashes. Each block contains the hash of the previous block, creating a continuous and immutable chain of records. This ensures that any attempt to alter a block would require changing all subsequent blocks, making tampering nearly impossible.
- **Nodes:**
    - Nodes are independent computers that maintain the blockchain. Each node has a copy of the entire blockchain and participates in the validation and relay of transactions.
    - Nodes communicate with each other to reach a consensus on the state of the blockchain, ensuring that all copies of the ledger are identical and up to date.

1.2 How It Works and Why It's Secure

Transaction Process:

- **Initiation:**
    - A transaction is initiated when a user requests to transfer an asset or record an event on the blockchain. This transaction is broadcasted to the network of nodes.
- **Verification:**
    - Network nodes verify the transaction using consensus algorithms. In Bitcoin's Proof-of-Work (PoW) system, miners compete to solve complex

mathematical problems to validate transactions. In Proof-of-Stake (PoS) systems, validators are chosen based on the number of coins they hold and are willing to "stake" as collateral.

- **Recording:**
  - Once verified, the transaction is added to a new block. This block is then proposed to the network for inclusion in the blockchain.
- **Linking:**
  - The new block is linked to the previous block using a cryptographic hash, forming a continuous and immutable chain. The hash of the previous block is included in the new block, ensuring the integrity of the chain.

Security Features:

- **Decentralization:**
  - The decentralized nature of blockchain means there is no single point of failure. Even if some nodes go offline or are compromised, the network continues to operate and maintain the integrity of the ledger.
- **Immutability:**
  - Once data is recorded in a block and added to the blockchain, it cannot be easily altered. This immutability is achieved through cryptographic hashing and the consensus mechanisms used to validate transactions. Any attempt to alter a block would require re-mining or re-validating all subsequent blocks, which is computationally infeasible.
- **Consensus Mechanisms:**
  - **Proof of Work (PoW):** Used by Bitcoin and many other cryptocurrencies, PoW requires miners to solve complex mathematical problems to validate transactions and create new blocks. This process is energy-intensive but ensures a high level of security.
  - **Proof of Stake (PoS):** PoS selects validators based on the number of coins they hold and are willing to

"stake" as collateral. This method is more energy-efficient than PoW and is used by cryptocurrencies like Ethereum 2.0 and Cardano .

This detailed section provides a comprehensive understanding of blockchain technology, its components, how it works, and why it is considered secure. It sets the stage for readers to grasp the fundamental principles that underpin cryptocurrencies and other blockchain-based applications.

Section 2: Types of Blockchains

2.1 Public vs. Private Blockchains

Public Blockchains:

- **Definition:**
  - Public blockchains are decentralized networks open to anyone who wishes to participate. They operate on a peer-to-peer network where all transactions are visible to everyone, ensuring transparency and trust among users.
- **Examples:**
  - **Bitcoin:** The first and most well-known public blockchain, created by Satoshi Nakamoto in 2009. Bitcoin operates as a decentralized digital currency, enabling peer-to-peer transactions without the need for a central authority.
  - **Ethereum:** Launched in 2015 by Vitalik Buterin, Ethereum introduced the concept of smart contracts—self-executing contracts with the terms directly written into code. Ethereum's blockchain supports decentralized applications (DApps), making it a versatile platform for various use cases.

- **Use Cases:**
  - **Cryptocurrencies:** Public blockchains are the foundation for cryptocurrencies like Bitcoin and Ethereum, enabling secure and transparent financial transactions.
  - **Public Decentralized Applications:** Ethereum's blockchain allows developers to create and deploy DApps that operate transparently and autonomously without central control. Examples include decentralized finance (DeFi) platforms, gaming applications, and supply chain management tools.

Private Blockchains:

- **Definition:**
  - Private blockchains are restricted networks controlled by a specific organization or group. Access to these blockchains is limited to authorized participants, providing greater control over the network and the data shared within it.
- **Examples:**
  - **Hyperledger:** An open-source collaborative effort hosted by the Linux Foundation. Hyperledger frameworks like Fabric and Sawtooth are designed for use by businesses to develop blockchain applications with modular architecture and high privacy levels.
  - **Corda:** Developed by R3, Corda is a blockchain platform specifically designed for the financial industry. It aims to streamline business transactions by enabling direct transactions between participants with high levels of security and privacy.
- **Use Cases:**
  - **Enterprise Solutions:** Private blockchains are used within organizations to enhance efficiency, security, and transparency in various business processes. They can be tailored to specific needs and regulatory requirements.

- o **Supply Chain Management:** Blockchain platforms like Hyperledger track and verify products throughout their lifecycle, providing an immutable record of the supply chain.
- o **Inter-Organizational Collaboration:** Platforms like Corda enable financial institutions to streamline agreements and contracts, reducing the need for intermediaries and increasing transaction speed and security.

2.2 Examples and Use Cases

Public Blockchain Use Cases:

- **Bitcoin:**
  - o **Digital Currency Transactions:** Bitcoin is primarily used for peer-to-peer digital currency transactions. It enables users to send and receive bitcoins without the need for a third-party intermediary, such as a bank. Bitcoin's blockchain provides a secure and transparent ledger for all transactions, ensuring trust and reliability.
- **Ethereum:**
  - o **Smart Contracts and DApps:** Ethereum's blockchain supports smart contracts, which are self-executing contracts where the terms of the agreement are written directly into code. This feature enables the creation of decentralized applications (DApps) that operate autonomously. Examples of DApps on Ethereum include DeFi platforms like Uniswap, which facilitate decentralized trading of cryptocurrencies, and gaming applications like CryptoKitties, where users can buy, sell, and breed digital cats.

Private Blockchain Use Cases:

- **Hyperledger in Supply Chain:**
  - **Track and Verify Products:** Hyperledger frameworks are used to track and verify products throughout their lifecycle in supply chains. For example, IBM's Food Trust platform, built on Hyperledger Fabric, enables participants in the food supply chain to trace the origin and journey of food products from farm to table. This enhances transparency, reduces fraud, and improves food safety.
- **Corda in Banking:**
  - **Streamline Financial Agreements:** Corda is designed to streamline financial agreements and contracts between institutions. It allows direct transactions between participating entities, eliminating the need for intermediaries and reducing transaction costs and time. For instance, banks use Corda to process cross-border payments more efficiently and securely.

This detailed section provides a comprehensive understanding of the different types of blockchains, their characteristics, and their use cases. It highlights the versatility of blockchain technology and its applications across various industries, setting the stage for readers to explore its potential in the world of cryptocurrency investing.

Section 3: Smart Contracts and Decentralized Applications (DApps)

3.1 Definition and Functionality

Smart Contracts:

- **Definition:**

- o Smart contracts are self-executing contracts with the terms of the agreement directly written into lines of code. These contracts are stored on a blockchain and automatically execute actions when predefined conditions are met.
- **How They Work:**
  - o When the conditions encoded in a smart contract are satisfied, the contract automatically enforces the agreed-upon terms without the need for intermediaries. For example, a smart contract for a crowdfunding campaign would automatically release funds to the project creator once the funding goal is reached, or return funds to contributors if the goal is not met .
- **Advantages:**
  - o **Automation:** Reduces the need for manual processing and intermediaries, saving time and costs.
  - o **Transparency:** All terms and conditions are visible on the blockchain, making the contract clear and verifiable by all parties.
  - o **Security:** The use of cryptographic security ensures that the contract cannot be tampered with once deployed.
  - o **Efficiency:** Automating contract execution reduces delays and potential errors associated with manual processing .

Decentralized Applications (DApps):

- **Definition:**
  - o DApps are applications that run on a blockchain network rather than on a single computer. They leverage the decentralized nature of blockchain to provide transparency, security, and autonomy .
- **Characteristics:**
  - o **Open Source:** DApps operate on open-source code that is publicly available, allowing anyone to inspect, use, and modify the application.

- **Incentivized:** DApps often include tokens that incentivize users and developers to participate and contribute to the network.
- **Consensus Mechanism:** DApps use blockchain consensus mechanisms like Proof of Work (PoW) or Proof of Stake (PoS) to validate transactions and ensure network security.

3.2 Real-World Applications

Smart Contract Applications:

- **Finance:**
  - **Automated Lending and Insurance:** Platforms like Aave and Compound use smart contracts to facilitate decentralized lending and borrowing. Users can lend their assets to earn interest or borrow against their holdings without a traditional intermediary. Smart contracts also enable automated insurance payouts based on predefined conditions.
- **Real Estate:**
  - **Simplified Property Transfers:** Smart contracts can automate and simplify property transactions by securely transferring ownership upon the fulfillment of specific conditions. Projects like Propy utilize blockchain to streamline real estate deals, reducing the need for intermediaries and paperwork.
- **Legal:**
  - **Transparent and Enforceable Agreements:** Smart contracts can be used to create legally binding agreements that automatically execute terms, reducing the potential for disputes. For example, Aragon provides tools for creating and managing decentralized organizations with enforceable governance structures encoded in smart contracts.

DApp Applications:

- **Decentralized Finance (DeFi):**
  - **Platforms like Uniswap:** Uniswap is a decentralized exchange (DEX) that allows users to trade cryptocurrencies directly from their wallets without relying on a centralized exchange. It uses automated market-making (AMM) algorithms to facilitate trades and provide liquidity.
- **Gaming:**
  - **Blockchain-Based Games like Axie Infinity:** Axie Infinity is a popular blockchain-based game where players collect, breed, and battle digital creatures called Axies. The game leverages Ethereum's blockchain to ensure the ownership and scarcity of Axies, allowing players to earn cryptocurrency by playing.
- **Social Media:**
  - **Platforms like Steemit:** Steemit is a blockchain-based social media platform where users earn cryptocurrency (STEEM) for creating and curating content. The platform incentivizes high-quality content creation and community engagement through a decentralized reward system.

This detailed section provides a comprehensive understanding of smart contracts and decentralized applications (DApps), showcasing their functionality and real-world applications. It highlights how these technologies leverage blockchain to create secure, transparent, and efficient solutions across various industries, setting the stage for readers to explore their potential in the cryptocurrency ecosystem.

Chapter 3: Setting Up for Success

Section 1: Choosing a Cryptocurrency Wallet

1.1 Types of Wallets (Hot vs. Cold)

Hot Wallets:

- **Definition:**
    - Hot wallets are digital wallets that are connected to the internet. They are used to store, send, and receive cryptocurrencies, providing easy access for users to manage their assets online.
- **Examples:**
    - **Mobile Wallets:**
        - **Trust Wallet:** A highly secure and user-friendly mobile wallet that supports a wide range of cryptocurrencies.
        - **Coinbase Wallet:** Offers robust security features and integration with the Coinbase exchange for easy management of assets.
    - **Desktop Wallets:**
        - **Exodus:** A popular desktop wallet with an intuitive interface and built-in exchange features.
        - **Electrum:** Known for its speed and low resource usage, suitable for Bitcoin transactions.
    - **Web Wallets:**
        - **MetaMask:** A browser extension wallet that supports Ethereum and ERC-20 tokens, commonly used for interacting with decentralized applications (DApps).
        - **Blockchain.info:** One of the oldest and most reliable web wallets, supporting multiple cryptocurrencies.
- **Advantages:**
    - **Easy Access and Convenience:** Hot wallets are ideal for frequent transactions and provide easy access to funds from anywhere with an internet connection.
    - **User-Friendly Interfaces:** Many hot wallets offer intuitive interfaces that are easy for beginners to navigate.

- **Disadvantages:**
  - **Higher Risk of Hacking and Online Threats:** Being connected to the internet makes hot wallets more susceptible to cyber attacks, phishing, and malware.
  - **Reliance on Security Measures:** Users must rely on the security protocols of the wallet provider, which can vary in effectiveness.

Cold Wallets:

- **Definition:**
  - Cold wallets are physical devices or paper-based storage methods that remain offline, making them less vulnerable to hacking and online threats. They are typically used for long-term storage of cryptocurrencies.
- **Examples:**
  - **Hardware Wallets:**
    - **Ledger Nano S:** A widely-used hardware wallet known for its high security and support for multiple cryptocurrencies.
    - **Trezor:** Another leading hardware wallet offering robust security features and ease of use.
  - **Paper Wallets:**
    - Printed QR codes of your public and private keys, allowing offline storage. These can be generated using tools like BitAddress or WalletGenerator.
- **Advantages:**
  - **Enhanced Security:** Cold wallets are offline and therefore protected from online attacks, making them ideal for storing large amounts of cryptocurrency over a long period.
  - **Control Over Private Keys:** Users retain full control over their private keys, ensuring that only they can access their funds.
- **Disadvantages:**

- **Less Convenient for Frequent Transactions:** The offline nature of cold wallets makes them less convenient for daily transactions.
- **Risk of Physical Loss or Damage:** Physical wallets can be lost, damaged, or stolen, which could result in the loss of the stored cryptocurrencies.

1.2 How to Set Up and Secure Your Wallet

Setting Up a Hot Wallet:

- **Download and Installation:**
  - Visit the official website or app store to download the wallet app. Ensure you are downloading from a legitimate source to avoid malicious software.
  - Install the app on your mobile device or desktop.
- **Creating an Account:**
  - Generate a new wallet address. This process will create a public key (address for receiving funds) and a private key (used for spending funds).
  - Backup your seed phrase—a series of words that can be used to recover your wallet if you lose access. Write this down and store it securely offline.
- **Security Measures:**
  - Enable two-factor authentication (2FA) for an added layer of security.
  - Create strong, unique passwords for your wallet and related accounts.
  - Regularly update the wallet software to protect against vulnerabilities.

Setting Up a Cold Wallet:

- **Purchasing and Initial Setup:**
  - Buy a hardware wallet from a reputable source, such as the official website of Ledger or Trezor. Avoid

purchasing from third-party sellers to prevent tampering.
  - Follow the manufacturer's instructions for initial configuration, which usually involves connecting the device to your computer and installing the necessary software.
- **Generating Keys:**
  - During setup, the hardware wallet will generate a private key and a public key. Write down the seed phrase provided and store it securely offline.
  - Never share your private key or seed phrase with anyone.
- **Usage Tips:**
  - Regularly update the firmware of your hardware wallet to protect against potential security flaws.
  - Store the physical device in a safe place to prevent loss or damage. Consider using a fireproof and waterproof safe for added protection.

General Security Practices:

- **Regular Backups:**
  - Keep multiple backups of your wallet's seed phrase in different secure locations. This ensures that you can recover your funds if one backup is lost or damaged.
- **Secure Storage:**
  - Use safe places such as safety deposit boxes or secure home safes to store your hardware wallets and paper wallets.
- **Staying Updated:**
  - Regularly update your wallet software and hardware firmware to protect against vulnerabilities and ensure you have the latest security features.
  - Stay informed about potential security threats and best practices for securing your digital assets.

This detailed section provides comprehensive guidance on choosing and setting up cryptocurrency wallets, ensuring that readers can securely manage their digital assets. By understanding the types of wallets and following best practices for security, beginners can confidently navigate the world of cryptocurrency investing.

Section 2: Understanding Cryptocurrency Exchanges

2.1 Centralized vs. Decentralized Exchanges

Centralized Exchanges (CEX):

- **Definition:**
    - Centralized exchanges (CEX) are platforms operated by companies that manage users' funds and transactions. These exchanges act as intermediaries between buyers and sellers, facilitating trades and maintaining custody of users' cryptocurrencies.
- **Examples:**
    - **Binance:** One of the largest cryptocurrency exchanges by trading volume, offering a wide range of cryptocurrencies and trading pairs.
    - **Coinbase:** A user-friendly platform popular among beginners, providing a secure environment for buying, selling, and storing cryptocurrencies.
    - **Kraken:** Known for its robust security features and comprehensive trading tools, Kraken caters to both novice and experienced traders.
- **Advantages:**
    - **High Liquidity:** Centralized exchanges typically have higher trading volumes and liquidity, making it easier to buy and sell cryptocurrencies quickly.
    - **User-Friendly Interfaces:** These platforms offer intuitive interfaces that simplify the trading process, making them accessible to beginners.

- - **Customer Support:** Centralized exchanges provide customer support services to assist users with any issues or questions.
- **Disadvantages:**
  - **Higher Security Risks:** Being centralized, these exchanges are prime targets for hackers. Notable incidents include the Mt. Gox and Coincheck hacks.
  - **Regulatory Scrutiny:** Centralized exchanges are subject to regulatory oversight, which can lead to account freezes or stricter KYC (Know Your Customer) requirements.

Decentralized Exchanges (DEX):

- **Definition:**
  - Decentralized exchanges (DEX) are peer-to-peer platforms that allow users to trade cryptocurrencies directly without an intermediary. Transactions are executed on the blockchain through smart contracts, enhancing security and privacy.
- **Examples:**
  - **Uniswap:** A leading DEX built on the Ethereum blockchain, known for its automated market-making (AMM) system.
  - **SushiSwap:** A community-driven DEX also based on Ethereum, offering various DeFi features beyond trading.
  - **PancakeSwap:** A popular DEX on the Binance Smart Chain, known for its low transaction fees and diverse range of tokens.
- **Advantages:**
  - **Enhanced Privacy:** DEX platforms do not require users to provide personal information, offering greater privacy and control over funds.
  - **Control Over Funds:** Users retain custody of their assets, reducing the risk of hacks and theft.
  - **Reduced Risk of Hacking:** The decentralized nature and lack of a central point of control make DEX platforms less susceptible to large-scale attacks.

- **Disadvantages:**
  - **Lower Liquidity:** DEX platforms generally have lower trading volumes and liquidity compared to centralized exchanges.
  - **More Complex Interfaces:** The user interfaces of DEX platforms can be more complex, posing a challenge for beginners.
  - **Limited Customer Support:** DEX platforms often lack customer support services, requiring users to resolve issues on their own.

2.2 How to Choose the Right Exchange for You

Factors to Consider:

- **Security:**
  - Investigate the exchange's reputation and history of security breaches. Look for platforms with robust security measures such as two-factor authentication (2FA), cold storage of funds, and regular security audits.
- **Fees:**
  - Compare trading fees, withdrawal fees, and other charges across different exchanges. Some platforms offer lower fees for high-volume traders or discounted rates for using the exchange's native token.
- **Supported Coins:**
  - Ensure the exchange supports the cryptocurrencies you wish to trade. Some exchanges offer a wide variety of tokens, while others may focus on a smaller selection.
- **User Experience:**
  - Evaluate the ease of use, customer support, and availability of a mobile app. User-friendly platforms can significantly enhance your trading experience, especially if you are new to cryptocurrency trading.

- **Liquidity:**
    - Higher liquidity ensures you can buy and sell cryptocurrencies quickly at market prices. Check the exchange's trading volume and market depth to assess liquidity.
- **Regulatory Compliance:**
    - Ensure the exchange complies with local laws and regulations. Look for platforms that require KYC verification to reduce the risk of fraud and ensure regulatory compliance.

Setting Up an Account:

- **Registration Process:**
    - Sign up for an account by providing your email address and creating a password. Some exchanges may require additional information for KYC verification, such as a government-issued ID and proof of address.
- **Funding Your Account:**
    - Deposit funds into your account using fiat currency or cryptocurrency. Most exchanges support various payment methods, including bank transfers, credit/debit cards, and other cryptocurrencies.
- **Making Your First Trade:**
    - Navigate the trading interface to select the cryptocurrency you wish to buy or sell. Place an order by choosing the type of order (market, limit, or stop-loss) and entering the amount. Review the details and confirm the trade.

This detailed section provides comprehensive guidance on understanding and choosing cryptocurrency exchanges. By considering the various factors and following the steps outlined, beginners can confidently select and use the right exchange to meet their trading needs.

Section 3: Regulations and Legal Considerations

3.1 Overview of Global Cryptocurrency Regulations

United States:

- **Regulatory Bodies:**
    - **SEC (Securities and Exchange Commission):** The SEC oversees securities transactions, ensuring that cryptocurrencies that qualify as securities comply with securities laws.
    - **CFTC (Commodity Futures Trading Commission):** The CFTC regulates commodity futures and options markets. It has classified Bitcoin and Ethereum as commodities, giving it authority over cryptocurrency derivatives trading.
    - **FinCEN (Financial Crimes Enforcement Network):** FinCEN monitors financial transactions to prevent money laundering and terrorist financing. It requires cryptocurrency exchanges to register as money services businesses (MSBs) and comply with anti-money laundering (AML) regulations.
- **Key Regulations:**
    - **Securities Laws:** Cryptocurrencies classified as securities must comply with SEC regulations, including registration and disclosure requirements.
    - **Anti-Money Laundering (AML) Policies:** Exchanges and other entities dealing in cryptocurrencies must implement AML policies, including customer due diligence and reporting suspicious activities.
    - **Tax Implications:** The IRS treats cryptocurrencies as property for tax purposes. This means capital gains taxes apply to cryptocurrency transactions, and accurate record-keeping is essential for tax reporting.

European Union:

- **Regulatory Bodies:**
    - **ESMA (European Securities and Markets Authority):** ESMA oversees securities markets and enforces securities regulations across EU member states, including those related to cryptocurrencies.
    - **EBA (European Banking Authority):** The EBA provides guidelines on the regulation of cryptocurrencies to ensure financial stability and consumer protection.
- **Key Regulations:**
    - **GDPR Compliance:** Cryptocurrency entities must comply with the General Data Protection Regulation (GDPR) to protect user data privacy.
    - **AMLD5 (5th Anti-Money Laundering Directive):** AMLD5 extends AML regulations to cryptocurrency exchanges and wallet providers, requiring them to register with authorities and conduct customer due diligence.

Asia:

- **Countries with Stringent Regulations:**
    - **China:** China has banned cryptocurrency exchanges and Initial Coin Offerings (ICOs) to prevent financial instability and capital flight. However, the country is actively developing its own central bank digital currency (CBDC), the digital yuan.
    - **India:** India has had a tumultuous regulatory environment for cryptocurrencies, with periods of uncertainty and potential bans. As of now, cryptocurrencies are not banned, but regulatory clarity is still evolving.
- **Crypto-Friendly Countries:**
    - **Japan:** The Financial Services Agency (FSA) regulates cryptocurrency exchanges, ensuring they comply with AML and investor protection laws.

Japan was one of the first countries to recognize Bitcoin as legal tender.
- **Singapore:** The Monetary Authority of Singapore (MAS) has created a favorable regulatory environment for cryptocurrencies, with clear guidelines and a proactive approach to fostering innovation in the fintech space.

Other Regions:

- **Adoption and Innovation:**
  - **Switzerland:** Known for its "Crypto Valley" in Zug, Switzerland has implemented blockchain-friendly regulations, making it a hub for cryptocurrency and blockchain startups. The Swiss Financial Market Supervisory Authority (FINMA) provides clear guidelines for ICOs and cryptocurrency businesses.
  - **Malta:** Malta has positioned itself as a "Blockchain Island" by implementing comprehensive regulations that attract cryptocurrency businesses. The Malta Financial Services Authority (MFSA) oversees the regulatory framework, ensuring compliance and promoting innovation.

3.2 Legal Issues and How to Stay Compliant

Taxation:

- **Reporting Requirements:**
  - Cryptocurrency investors must report their earnings, capital gains, and losses to tax authorities. This includes documenting the acquisition, sale, exchange, or any other disposition of cryptocurrency.
  - **Tools and Resources:** Utilizing crypto tax software like CoinTracker, Koinly, or TokenTax can help streamline the process of calculating gains and preparing tax reports. Consulting with a tax

professional knowledgeable in cryptocurrency regulations is also advisable.

Anti-Money Laundering (AML) and Know Your Customer (KYC):

- **Compliance:**
    - Exchanges and other cryptocurrency service providers must implement robust AML and KYC procedures to verify the identities of their customers and monitor transactions for suspicious activities.
    - **Importance:** These measures help prevent money laundering, terrorist financing, and other illicit activities, ensuring the integrity and security of the financial system.

Staying Informed:

- **Monitoring Regulations:**
    - Cryptocurrency regulations are continually evolving. Investors and businesses must stay informed about changes in laws and regulations to remain compliant and avoid legal issues.
    - **Legal Advice:** For complex issues or significant investments, seeking professional legal advice from attorneys specializing in cryptocurrency and blockchain law is recommended. They can provide tailored guidance and help navigate the regulatory landscape.

Chapter 3 of "Crypto for Beginners: A Step-by-Step Guide to Digital Currency Investing" provides detailed guidance on setting up and securing cryptocurrency wallets, understanding and choosing the right cryptocurrency exchanges, and navigating the regulatory landscape to ensure compliance and informed investing. This section equips readers with the knowledge to navigate the complex legal environment surrounding cryptocurrencies, helping them to stay compliant and make informed investment decisions.

Chapter 4: Investment Strategies

Section 1: Long-Term Holding (HODLing) vs. Active Trading

1.1 Long-Term Holding (HODLing)

Definition:

- **HODLing:** HODLing, a term derived from a misspelled "hold" in a 2013 Bitcoin forum post, refers to the strategy of buying cryptocurrencies and holding them for an extended period, regardless of market fluctuations. This approach is based on the belief that, despite short-term volatility, the value of cryptocurrencies will increase significantly over time.

Benefits:

- **Potential for Significant Appreciation:**
    - Historical data shows that long-term holders of Bitcoin and Ethereum have seen substantial gains. For example, Bitcoin, which was worth less than $1 in 2010, reached an all-time high of over $68,000 in November 2021. As of June 2024, Bitcoin's value hovers around $70,000.
    - Ethereum, launched in 2015 at around $0.30, surpassed $4,800 in November 2021.
- **Reduced Transaction Costs:**
    - HODLing minimizes transaction costs as it involves fewer trades compared to active trading. Each trade incurs fees, which can add up quickly with frequent trading.
- **Lower Stress from Daily Market Monitoring:**
    - HODLers are less concerned with daily market movements and short-term volatility. This approach

reduces the stress and emotional strain associated with constant market monitoring.

Challenges:

- **Requires Patience and Resilience to Market Volatility:**
  - The cryptocurrency market is known for its extreme volatility. Long-term holders must be patient and resilient, enduring significant price swings without panic selling.
- **Risk of Prolonged Downturns:**
  - There is always a risk that a prolonged market downturn could negatively impact the value of held assets. For example, Bitcoin experienced an 80% drop in value during the 2018 bear market, testing the resolve of long-term holders.

Examples:

- **Bitcoin (BTC):** Bitcoin's price has shown a general upward trend over the years, rewarding those who have held onto it despite volatility.
- **Ethereum (ETH):** Ethereum's growth has mirrored Bitcoin's, with substantial gains for long-term holders, especially given its role in the burgeoning DeFi and NFT markets.

1.2 Active Trading

Definition:

- **Active Trading:** Active trading involves frequently buying and selling cryptocurrencies to capitalize on short-term market movements. This strategy requires a keen understanding of the market and a readiness to act quickly.

Types of Trading:

- **Day Trading:** Buying and selling within the same day to profit from intraday price movements.
- **Swing Trading:** Holding positions for several days or weeks to capitalize on expected price movements.
- **Scalping:** Making multiple trades within a day to profit from small price changes.

Benefits:

- **Potential for Quick Profits:**
    o Active trading can yield significant profits in a short time if done correctly. Traders can capitalize on daily volatility to make quick gains.
- **Opportunities to Capitalize on Market Volatility:**
    o The high volatility of the cryptocurrency market presents numerous opportunities for traders to profit from price swings.

Challenges:

- **Requires Time, Expertise, and Constant Market Monitoring:**
    o Successful active trading demands a deep understanding of market trends, technical analysis, and constant monitoring of the market.
    o It requires significant time investment and expertise to make informed trading decisions.
- **Higher Transaction Costs:**
    o Frequent trading incurs higher transaction fees, which can erode profits. Each trade involves fees that can add up, especially on high-frequency trading platforms.
- **Increased Stress:**
    o The need to constantly monitor the market and make rapid decisions can lead to increased stress and emotional strain.

1.2 Diversification and Risk Management

Diversification:

Definition:

- **Diversification:** Spreading investments across various cryptocurrencies to reduce risk. This strategy ensures that a poor performance by one asset does not disproportionately affect the overall portfolio.

Benefits:

- **Mitigates Risk of a Single Asset's Poor Performance:**
  - Diversification reduces the impact of any one asset's poor performance on the overall portfolio. By holding a variety of cryptocurrencies, investors can spread their risk.
- **Exposure to Different Sectors and Innovations:**
  - Investing in different cryptocurrencies exposes investors to various sectors and innovations within the blockchain ecosystem, such as DeFi, NFTs, and enterprise blockchain solutions.

Strategies:

- **Investing in a Mix of Large-Cap and Small-Cap Cryptocurrencies:**
  - Large-cap cryptocurrencies like Bitcoin and Ethereum are generally more stable and less volatile. Small-cap cryptocurrencies, while riskier, can offer higher returns. A balanced mix can optimize the risk-reward ratio.
- **Including Tokens from Different Blockchain Platforms:**
  - Diversifying across various blockchain platforms (e.g., Ethereum, Binance Smart Chain, Solana) can mitigate risks associated with any single platform's potential issues or failures.

Risk Management:

Strategies:

- **Setting Stop-Loss Orders:**
    - Stop-loss orders automatically sell a cryptocurrency when it reaches a certain price, limiting potential losses.
- **Position Sizing:**
    - Proper position sizing involves determining the appropriate amount to invest in each trade or asset, based on the overall portfolio size and risk tolerance.
- **Regular Portfolio Rebalancing:**
    - Regularly adjusting the portfolio to maintain the desired level of risk and ensure alignment with investment goals.

Risk Assessment:

- **Evaluating Volatility and Historical Performance:**
    - Assessing the volatility and historical performance of each cryptocurrency helps in understanding potential risks and making informed investment decisions.
- **Understanding Market Conditions:**
    - Keeping abreast of market conditions, news, and developments in the cryptocurrency space is crucial for effective risk management.

This detailed section provides a comprehensive guide to different investment strategies in the cryptocurrency market. By understanding the nuances of long-term holding versus active trading, and the importance of diversification and risk management, beginners can make informed decisions to optimize their investment portfolios.

Section 2: Analysing Cryptocurrencies

2.1 Fundamental Analysis

Overview:

- **Purpose:**
  - Fundamental analysis aims to assess the intrinsic value of a cryptocurrency. This involves evaluating various aspects of the cryptocurrency to determine whether it is overvalued, undervalued, or fairly valued based on its current price.
- **Key Factors:**
  - **Technology:** The robustness, innovation, and scalability of the underlying blockchain technology.
  - **Team:** The experience, skills, and track record of the founders and developers.
  - **Use Case:** The real-world applications and problems the cryptocurrency aims to solve.
  - **Partnerships:** Strategic alliances and collaborations with other companies and projects.
  - **Market Demand:** The current and potential future demand for the cryptocurrency.

Technology and Innovation:

- **Blockchain:**
  - Assessing the blockchain's underlying technology includes understanding its consensus mechanism (e.g., Proof of Work, Proof of Stake), scalability (ability to handle a growing amount of work or transactions), and security features. For example, Ethereum's transition to Ethereum 2.0 aims to improve scalability and energy efficiency through Proof of Stake.
- **Development Activity:**

- Monitoring development activity provides insights into the project's progress and commitment. This can be done by reviewing GitHub repositories for the number of commits, contributors, and updates. Active development often indicates a healthy and continuously improving project.

Team and Partnerships:

- **Founders and Developers:**
  - The background and experience of the team behind a cryptocurrency can significantly influence its potential success. For instance, Ethereum's creator, Vitalik Buterin, is a well-respected figure in the crypto community, lending credibility to the project.
- **Partnerships:**
  - Strategic alliances and collaborations can enhance a cryptocurrency's adoption and development. For example, Ripple's (XRP) partnerships with major financial institutions like Santander and American Express have boosted its credibility and use case for cross-border payments.

Market Demand and Adoption:

- **Use Case:**
  - Evaluating the cryptocurrency's use case involves understanding its real-world applications and problem-solving capabilities. Cryptocurrencies like Bitcoin are seen as a store of value, while Ethereum is used for decentralized applications (DApps) and smart contracts.
- **Adoption Metrics:**
  - Adoption metrics include the number of users, transaction volume, and community engagement. High adoption rates and active communities can indicate a strong market presence and future growth potential. Websites like CoinMarketCap and

CoinGecko provide data on transaction volumes and user activity.

2.2 Technical Analysis

Overview:

- **Purpose:**
    - Technical analysis focuses on analysing price movements and market trends to make trading decisions. It involves studying historical data to predict future price movements based on patterns and indicators.
- **Tools and Indicators:**
    - Technical analysis uses various charts, patterns, and technical indicators to provide insights into market behavior and potential price movements.

Key Indicators:

- **Moving Averages (MA):**
    - **Simple Moving Average (SMA):** Calculated by averaging the closing prices over a specified period. It helps identify the direction of the trend.
    - **Exponential Moving Average (EMA):** Gives more weight to recent prices, making it more responsive to new information. It is useful for identifying short-term trends.
- **Relative Strength Index (RSI):**
    - The RSI measures the speed and change of price movements. It ranges from 0 to 100, with values above 70 indicating overbought conditions and below 30 indicating oversold conditions. It helps identify potential reversal points.
- **Moving Average Convergence Divergence (MACD):**
    - The MACD is a trend-following indicator that shows the relationship between two moving averages of a

cryptocurrency's price. It consists of the MACD line, signal line, and histogram. The MACD can help identify changes in the strength, direction, momentum, and duration of a trend .

Chart Patterns:

- **Candlestick Patterns:**
    - **Doji:** Indicates indecision in the market and potential reversal points.
    - **Hammer:** A bullish reversal pattern that forms after a downtrend.
    - **Engulfing Patterns:** Bullish or bearish patterns that signal potential reversals .
- **Trend Patterns:**
    - **Head and Shoulders:** Indicates a potential reversal of a current trend.
    - **Double Tops and Bottoms:** Signal the end of a trend and a possible reversal.
    - **Triangles (Ascending, Descending, Symmetrical):** Continuation patterns that indicate potential breakout directions
-
- Here is the technical analysis chart showing key indicators such as Simple Moving Average (SMA), Exponential Moving Average (EMA), Relative Strength Index (RSI), and Moving Average Convergence Divergence (MACD), along with candlestick patterns like Doji, Hammer, and Engulfing Patterns, and trend patterns like Head and Shoulders, Double Tops and Bottoms, and Triangles.
- This image illustrates the various tools and indicators used in technical analysis, providing a visual representation to help beginners understand how to analyse cryptocurrency price movements and market trends.

2.3 Sentiment Analysis

Overview:

- **Purpose:**
  - Sentiment analysis gauges the overall mood and sentiment in the market to predict potential market movements. It helps traders understand the emotional state of the market participants, which can drive price movements.
- **Sources:**
  - Sentiment analysis gathers data from various sources, including social media, news, forums, and specialized sentiment analysis tools.

Methods:

- **Social Media Monitoring:**
    - Analysing discussions and trends on platforms like Twitter, Reddit, and Telegram provides insights into the market sentiment. Positive or negative sentiment on these platforms can influence market behavior.
- **News Analysis:**
    - Keeping track of major news events and their impact on the market is crucial. News related to regulatory changes, technological advancements, partnerships, and market trends can significantly affect cryptocurrency prices.
- **Sentiment Tools:**
    - Using AI and machine learning tools, such as The TIE and LunarCrush, to assess overall market sentiment. These tools analyse large volumes of data to provide sentiment scores and trends.

This detailed section provides a comprehensive guide to analysing cryptocurrencies. By understanding fundamental, technical, and sentiment analysis, beginners can make informed decisions and develop effective investment strategies in the cryptocurrency market.

Section 3: Building Your Crypto Portfolio

3.1 Steps to Create a Balanced Portfolio

Assessing Risk Tolerance:

- **Self-Evaluation:**
    - Determining your comfort level with risk, investment horizon, and financial goals is crucial in building a balanced cryptocurrency portfolio. This involves understanding how much volatility you can handle, the duration for which you can invest without needing to liquidate your assets, and your overall financial objectives.
    - **Risk Categories:**

- **Conservative:** Suitable for investors who prefer low-risk investments with stable returns. Conservative portfolios focus on minimizing risk and protecting capital.
- **Balanced:** Designed for investors willing to take moderate risks to achieve higher returns. These portfolios balance stability and growth.
- **Aggressive:** Targeted at investors who are comfortable with high levels of risk in pursuit of significant returns. Aggressive portfolios focus on growth and include high-risk assets.

Asset Allocation:

- **Core Holdings:**
    - **Bitcoin (BTC):** Often considered the gold standard of cryptocurrencies, Bitcoin provides stability and is less volatile compared to smaller cryptocurrencies. It constitutes the core of many crypto portfolios.
    - **Ethereum (ETH):** Known for its smart contract capabilities and wide adoption in decentralized applications (DApps), Ethereum offers both stability and growth potential.
- **Growth Assets:**
    - **Smaller-Cap Cryptocurrencies:** Investing in smaller-cap cryptocurrencies and emerging projects can yield high returns. These assets are more volatile but offer significant upside potential.
    - **Examples:** Polkadot (DOT), Solana (SOL), and Chainlink (LINK) are popular choices for growth assets.
- **Income-Generating Assets:**
    - **Staking Coins:** Cryptocurrencies that offer staking rewards allow investors to earn passive income by participating in the network's consensus mechanism.
    - **Yield Farming Tokens:** DeFi platforms offer yield farming opportunities where investors can lend or provide liquidity to earn interest or additional tokens.

Regular Rebalancing:

- **Monitoring Performance:**
    - Regularly reviewing the performance of your portfolio and keeping an eye on market conditions is essential for maintaining a balanced portfolio. This involves tracking the value of your investments and assessing their alignment with your financial goals.
- **Adjusting Allocation:**
    - Rebalancing your portfolio involves adjusting your asset allocation to maintain your desired risk exposure and capitalize on new opportunities. This can include selling assets that have performed well and reallocating funds to underperforming or new promising investments.

3.2 Example Portfolios for Different Risk Tolerances

Conservative Portfolio:

- **Allocation:**
    - **70% Bitcoin (BTC):** Provides stability and long-term growth potential.
    - **20% Ethereum (ETH):** Adds exposure to smart contracts and DeFi while maintaining relative stability.
    - **10% Stablecoins:** Such as USDT or USDC, provide liquidity and protection against market volatility.
- **Objective:**
    - Minimize risk while achieving steady growth. This portfolio focuses on well-established cryptocurrencies and stable assets to preserve capital and ensure low volatility.

Balanced Portfolio:

- **Allocation:**

- - **50% Bitcoin (BTC):** Core holding for stability and growth.
  - **25% Ethereum (ETH):** Significant exposure to DeFi and DApps.
  - **15% Other Top-20 Cryptocurrencies:** Such as Binance Coin (BNB), Cardano (ADA), and Ripple (XRP), for diversification.
  - **10% DeFi Tokens:** Such as Uniswap (UNI) and Aave (AAVE), to capitalize on the growing DeFi sector.
- **Objective:**
  - Balanced risk with exposure to growth opportunities. This portfolio aims to achieve higher returns while maintaining a moderate level of risk through diversified holdings.

Aggressive Portfolio:

- **Allocation:**
  - **30% Bitcoin (BTC):** Core holding for some stability.
  - **20% Ethereum (ETH):** Exposure to the leading smart contract platform.
  - **30% Small-Cap Cryptocurrencies:** Such as Polkadot (DOT), Solana (SOL), and Avalanche (AVAX), which have high growth potential.
  - **20% High-Risk/High-Reward Tokens:** Including new and emerging projects, ICOs, and high-yield DeFi tokens.
- **Objective:**
  - Maximize potential returns with higher risk exposure. This portfolio targets significant gains through investments in volatile and high-growth assets.

Chapter 4 of "Crypto for Beginners: A Step-by-Step Guide to Digital Currency Investing" provides detailed guidance on various investment strategies, methods for analysing cryptocurrencies, and steps to build a balanced and diversified crypto portfolio tailored to different risk tolerances. This comprehensive approach ensures that beginners are well-equipped to make informed investment decisions in the cryptocurrency market.

Chapter 5: Trading Cryptocurrencies

Section 1: Introduction to Crypto Trading

1.1 Basic Trading Concepts

Cryptocurrency Trading:

- **Definition and Overview of Trading Digital Assets:**
  - Cryptocurrency trading involves buying and selling digital assets through various exchanges to profit from market movements. Traders aim to capitalize on the price fluctuations of cryptocurrencies like Bitcoin, Ethereum, and other altcoins.
  - Unlike long-term investors who focus on holding assets for extended periods, traders frequently enter and exit positions to exploit short-term price changes.
- **Differences Between Cryptocurrency Trading and Traditional Stock Trading:**
  - **Market Hours:** Traditional stock markets have set trading hours, typically from 9:30 AM to 4:00 PM EST on weekdays. In contrast, cryptocurrency markets operate 24/7, allowing traders to execute trades at any time, including weekends and holidays.
  - **Volatility:** Cryptocurrencies are known for their high volatility compared to traditional stocks. Significant price swings can occur within minutes or hours, offering both opportunities and risks for traders.
  - **Regulation:** Stock markets are heavily regulated by government bodies like the SEC (Securities and Exchange Commission) in the US. Cryptocurrency markets, however, are less regulated, leading to

different dynamics and potential risks, such as market manipulation.

Market Participants:

- **Retail Traders:**
    - Individual investors who trade with their own capital. Retail traders often use online exchanges and trading platforms to buy and sell cryptocurrencies.
    - Impact: Retail traders contribute to market liquidity and can drive price movements, especially in smaller-cap cryptocurrencies.
- **Institutional Investors:**
    - Large entities such as hedge funds, investment firms, and corporate treasuries that trade significant amounts of capital. Institutional investors often employ sophisticated trading strategies and have access to advanced trading tools.
    - Impact: Their large trades can significantly impact market prices and liquidity. The entry of institutional investors has contributed to the maturation of the cryptocurrency market.
- **Market Makers:**
    - Entities or individuals that provide liquidity to the market by placing buy and sell orders. Market makers earn a profit from the bid-ask spread and help reduce price volatility.
    - Impact: By providing liquidity, market makers ensure smoother price movements and reduce the spread between buying and selling prices.
- **Whales:**
    - Individual or institutional investors who hold large quantities of cryptocurrency. Their trades can significantly influence market prices due to the volume of assets they control.
    - Impact: Whales can cause substantial price swings if they decide to buy or sell large amounts of cryptocurrency, leading to potential market manipulation.

1.2 Types of Orders

Market Orders:

- **Definition:**
    - A market order is an order to buy or sell a cryptocurrency immediately at the current market price. It guarantees execution but not the exact price.
- **Advantages:**
    - **Quick Execution:** Market orders are executed instantly, making them ideal for entering or exiting positions rapidly.
    - **Simplicity:** Easy to use and understand, suitable for beginners and situations where immediate execution is crucial.
- **Disadvantages:**
    - **Risk of Slippage:** In highly volatile markets, the executed price can be significantly different from the expected price due to rapid price changes between placing the order and its execution.

Limit Orders:

- **Definition:**
    - A limit order is an order to buy or sell a cryptocurrency at a specific price or better. A buy limit order will only execute at the limit price or lower, while a sell limit order will only execute at the limit price or higher.
- **Advantages:**
    - **Control Over Price:** Provides control over the entry or exit price, ensuring that trades are executed at a desirable price.
    - **Useful in Volatile Markets:** Helps manage the impact of volatility by setting price limits for trades.
- **Disadvantages:**

- o **Potential Non-Execution:** If the market does not reach the specified price, the order will not be executed, potentially missing trading opportunities.

Stop-Loss Orders:

- **Definition:**
  - o A stop-loss order is an order to sell a cryptocurrency when it reaches a certain price. It is used to limit potential losses by automatically selling an asset at a predetermined price.
- **Advantages:**
  - o **Risk Management Tool:** Helps prevent significant losses by ensuring that positions are closed before losses become too large.
  - o **Automated Protection:** Provides automated protection against adverse price movements without the need for constant market monitoring.
- **Disadvantages:**
  - o **Potential for False Breakouts:** Stop-loss orders can be triggered by short-term market fluctuations, leading to the sale of assets during temporary price drops (false breakouts).

(

Chapter 5 of "Crypto for Beginners: A Step-by-Step Guide to Digital Currency Investing" introduces readers to the basics of cryptocurrency trading. This section covers fundamental trading concepts, the different market participants, and the various types of orders used in trading. By understanding these concepts, beginners can develop a solid foundation for their trading activities in the dynamic cryptocurrency market.

Section 2: Technical Analysis Tools

2.1 Chart Patterns and Indicators

Candlestick Patterns:

- **Doji:**
    - **Definition:** A Doji candlestick forms when the opening and closing prices are virtually the same, creating a thin or non-existent body. This pattern indicates indecision in the market, where neither buyers nor sellers dominate.
    - **Significance:** A Doji can signal a potential reversal in the market trend. For instance, after a prolonged uptrend, a Doji may suggest that buying pressure is weakening, potentially leading to a downtrend.
    - **Example:** A Doji appearing after a series of bullish candles might indicate that the upward momentum is slowing down.
- **Hammer:**
    - **Definition:** A Hammer candlestick features a small body at the upper end of the trading range and a long lower shadow. It typically appears at the bottom of a downtrend.
    - **Significance:** This pattern suggests that despite selling pressure during the trading session, buyers managed to push the price back up, signaling a potential price increase.
    - **Example:** A Hammer appearing after a downtrend might indicate a bullish reversal, where buyers start to take control.
- **Engulfing Patterns:**
    - **Definition:** Engulfing patterns occur when a candlestick fully engulfs the previous candlestick's body. There are bullish and bearish engulfing patterns.
    - **Bullish Engulfing:** A small bearish candle followed by a larger bullish candle. Indicates potential upward reversal.

- **Bearish Engulfing:** A small bullish candle followed by a larger bearish candle. Indicates potential downward reversal.
- **Example:** In a downtrend, a bullish engulfing pattern suggests that buying pressure is strong enough to reverse the trend.

Trend Patterns:

- **Head and Shoulders:**
  - **Definition:** This reversal pattern consists of three peaks: a higher peak (head) between two lower peaks (shoulders). It signals a potential trend change from bullish to bearish.
  - **Example:** After an uptrend, a Head and Shoulders pattern might indicate that the price is likely to decline.
- **Double Tops and Bottoms:**
  - **Double Top:** Formed by two consecutive peaks at roughly the same price level. Indicates potential bearish reversal.
  - **Double Bottom:** Formed by two consecutive troughs at roughly the same price level. Indicates potential bullish reversal.
  - **Example:** A Double Top after an uptrend suggests that the asset might face resistance and reverse into a downtrend.
- **Triangles (Ascending, Descending, Symmetrical):**
  - **Ascending Triangle:** Formed by a horizontal resistance line and an upward sloping support line. Indicates a potential bullish breakout.
  - **Descending Triangle:** Formed by a horizontal support line and a downward sloping resistance line. Indicates a potential bearish breakout.
  - **Symmetrical Triangle:** Formed by converging trendlines. Indicates potential breakout in either direction.
  - **Example:** An Ascending Triangle during an uptrend can suggest that the price will likely break upwards.

2.2 Using Tools like Moving Averages, RSI, MACD

Moving Averages (MA):

- **Simple Moving Average (SMA):**
    - **Definition:** The SMA is calculated by averaging the closing prices over a specified period. It smoothens out price data to identify the direction of the trend.
    - **Applications:** Used to identify trend direction and potential support or resistance levels. A common strategy is the "Golden Cross" where a short-term SMA crosses above a long-term SMA, indicating a potential buy signal.
    - **Example:** A 50-day SMA crossing above the 200-day SMA can signal the beginning of an uptrend.
- **Exponential Moving Average (EMA):**
    - **Definition:** The EMA gives more weight to recent prices, making it more responsive to new information.
    - **Applications:** Used for identifying trends and potential reversal points. EMA is particularly useful in volatile markets.
    - **Example:** Traders might use the 12-day and 26-day EMA to generate buy or sell signals.

Relative Strength Index (RSI):

- **Definition:** RSI is a momentum oscillator that measures the speed and change of price movements. It ranges from 0 to 100.
    - **Scale:** Values above 70 typically indicate overbought conditions, while values below 30 indicate oversold conditions.
    - **Applications:** RSI helps identify potential reversal points and confirm trends. An RSI divergence (price makes a new high but RSI does not) can signal a potential trend reversal.

- **Example:** An RSI dropping below 30 might indicate that the asset is oversold and could be due for a price correction.

Moving Average Convergence Divergence (MACD):

- **Components:**
  - **MACD Line:** Difference between the 12-day and 26-day EMA.
  - **Signal Line:** 9-day EMA of the MACD line.
  - **Histogram:** Difference between the MACD line and the Signal line.
  - **Applications:** MACD is used to identify the direction and strength of a trend and potential reversal points. A common strategy is the MACD crossover, where the MACD line crossing above the Signal line indicates a potential buy signal.
  - **Example:** A bullish crossover (MACD line crossing above the Signal line) can suggest the start of an upward trend.

Chapter 5 of "Crypto for Beginners: A Step-by-Step Guide to Digital Currency Investing" provides detailed insights into technical analysis tools. This section covers chart patterns and indicators, including how to use Moving Averages, RSI, and MACD effectively. By understanding these tools, beginners can make more informed trading decisions in the dynamic cryptocurrency market.

Section 3: Developing a Trading Plan

3.1 Setting Goals and Limits

Defining Trading Objectives:

- **Short-Term vs. Long-Term Goals:**

- **Short-Term Goals:** These are objectives that you aim to achieve within a shorter time frame, such as a few days to a few weeks. Short-term trading often involves day trading or swing trading strategies, where the goal is to capitalize on short-term price movements.
- **Long-Term Goals:** Long-term trading objectives span several months to years. This involves holding onto assets for extended periods, often with the belief that the asset will appreciate significantly over time. Long-term goals align more with HODLing and investment strategies.

- **Financial Targets and Acceptable Levels of Risk:**
    - **Financial Targets:** Clearly define your financial goals, such as a specific profit percentage or a monetary gain. For example, a trader might aim for a 10% monthly return on their investment.
    - **Acceptable Levels of Risk:** Determine the maximum amount of capital you are willing to risk on a single trade. This involves setting risk tolerance levels that align with your financial situation and comfort with potential losses.

Risk Management:

- **Position Sizing:**
    - **Definition:** Position sizing involves determining the appropriate amount of capital to allocate to each trade. It helps manage risk by ensuring that no single trade has the potential to significantly impact the overall portfolio.
    - **Methodology:** A common method is the 1% rule, where a trader risks no more than 1% of their total capital on a single trade. For example, if you have $10,000 in your trading account, you would risk no more than $100 on any one trade.
- **Setting Stop-Loss and Take-Profit Levels:**
    - **Stop-Loss Orders:** These are predetermined price levels at which a trade will be automatically sold to

prevent further losses. Setting a stop-loss order helps protect your capital by limiting the amount you can lose on a trade.
- **Take-Profit Orders:** These are predetermined price levels at which a trade will be automatically sold to secure profits. Take-profit orders help ensure that you lock in gains once a trade reaches a favorable price.

3.2 Keeping Track of Your Trades and Performance

Trade Journal:

- **Importance of Maintaining a Detailed Record:**
  - Keeping a trade journal is essential for tracking your trading activities and improving your strategies. It allows you to review past trades, analyse your performance, and learn from both successful and unsuccessful trades.
  - **Components of a Trade Journal:**
    - **Entry and Exit Points:** Record the price at which you enter and exit each trade.
    - **Position Sizes:** Note the amount of capital allocated to each trade.
    - **Trade Outcomes:** Document the results of each trade, including profits or losses.
    - **Reasons for Each Trade:** Write down the rationale behind each trade decision, such as technical indicators, market news, or trading signals.

Performance Analysis:

- **Regularly Reviewing Trade History:**
  - Periodically review your trade history to identify patterns and areas for improvement. This involves analysing the data in your trade journal to understand your trading behavior and performance.

- **Metrics to Monitor:**
    - **Win/Loss Ratio:** The number of winning trades divided by the number of losing trades. A higher ratio indicates a higher success rate.
    - **Average Profit/Loss per Trade:** The average amount gained or lost on each trade. This helps assess the overall profitability of your trading strategy.
    - **Maximum Drawdown:** The largest peak-to-trough decline in your portfolio value. It measures the maximum loss from the highest portfolio value to the lowest.

Continuous Learning and Adaptation:

- **Staying Updated with Market News and Developments:**
    - The cryptocurrency market is dynamic and constantly evolving. Staying informed about market news, regulatory changes, technological advancements, and major events is crucial for making informed trading decisions.
    - **Adapting Trading Strategies:**
        - Based on performance analysis and market conditions, adjust your trading strategies to improve results. This might involve changing your risk management approach, using different technical indicators, or exploring new trading techniques.

Chapter 5 of "Crypto for Beginners: A Step-by-Step Guide to Digital Currency Investing" provides comprehensive guidance on the fundamentals of crypto trading, essential technical analysis tools, and developing a robust trading plan. This ensures that beginners are well-equipped to navigate the complexities of cryptocurrency trading and make informed decisions to achieve their financial goals.

Chapter 6: Staying Informed and Safe

Section 1: Crypto News and Resources

1.1 Reliable Sources for Cryptocurrency News

News Websites:

- **CoinDesk:**
    - **Overview:** CoinDesk is a leading news platform that covers blockchain technology, digital assets, and cryptocurrency news. Founded in 2013, it provides timely and comprehensive updates on the crypto market, regulatory developments, and industry trends.
    - **Content:** CoinDesk publishes daily news articles, market analysis, research reports, and opinion pieces from industry experts. It also hosts the annual Consensus conference, one of the largest events in the cryptocurrency space.
    - **Website:** CoinDesk
- **CoinTelegraph:**
    - **Overview:** CoinTelegraph is another major source for cryptocurrency news, offering a wide range of articles, updates, and market analysis. It covers all aspects of the crypto industry, from price movements to regulatory news and technological advancements.
    - **Content:** CoinTelegraph features daily news, in-depth articles, interviews with industry leaders, and educational content aimed at both beginners and advanced users.
    - **Website:** CoinTelegraph
- **CryptoSlate:**
    - **Overview:** CryptoSlate provides news, data, and real-time information about the blockchain and cryptocurrency industry. It is known for its comprehensive coverage and detailed market data.
    - **Content:** CryptoSlate offers breaking news, market analysis, project reviews, and a directory of

blockchain companies and products. It also includes educational resources for new investors.
- Website: CryptoSlate

Market Data Platforms:

- **CoinMarketCap:**
    - **Overview:** CoinMarketCap is a widely-used platform that provides detailed market data, prices, and charts for various cryptocurrencies. It is considered one of the most reliable sources for tracking cryptocurrency market capitalization and rankings.
    - **Content:** Users can access real-time price updates, historical data, trading volume, market cap, and detailed information on each listed cryptocurrency.
    - **Website:** CoinMarketCap
- **CryptoCompare:**
    - **Overview:** CryptoCompare offers comprehensive data, charts, and portfolio tracking tools for cryptocurrency investors. It provides detailed information on exchanges, trading pairs, and market trends.
    - **Content:** The platform includes market data, price comparisons, mining information, and reviews of wallets and exchanges. It also features a portfolio tracking tool for users to manage their investments.
    - **Website:** CryptoCompare

Official Blogs and Websites:

- **Bitcoin.org:**
    - **Overview:** Bitcoin.org is the official website for Bitcoin information and updates. It was originally registered by Bitcoin's pseudonymous creator, Satoshi Nakamoto, and is now maintained by the Bitcoin community.
    - **Content:** The site offers educational resources, news updates, and guides on how to use and secure Bitcoin.

It also includes a section for developers with technical documentation and software releases.
- **Website:** Bitcoin.org
- **Ethereum.org:**
    - **Overview:** Ethereum.org is the official site for Ethereum, providing updates, resources, and development news. It serves as a hub for information about the Ethereum blockchain and its applications.
    - **Content:** Ethereum.org features educational content, developer resources, information on Ethereum projects and use cases, and updates on the Ethereum network's development and upgrades.
    - **Website:** Ethereum.org

1.2 Community Forums and Educational Resources

Community Forums:

- **Reddit:**
    - **Overview:** Reddit hosts a number of subreddits dedicated to cryptocurrency discussions, news, and community support.
    - **Popular Subreddits:**
        - **r/Bitcoin:** Discussions on Bitcoin-related topics, news, and updates.
        - **r/Ethereum:** Focused on Ethereum and its ecosystem, including DApps and smart contracts.
        - **r/Cryptocurrency:** General discussions on all aspects of the cryptocurrency market.
    - **Website:** Reddit
- **BitcoinTalk:**
    - **Overview:** BitcoinTalk is one of the oldest forums dedicated to Bitcoin and other cryptocurrencies. It was created by Satoshi Nakamoto in 2009 and remains a key platform for discussions and announcements.

- **Content:** The forum covers a wide range of topics, including Bitcoin development, market analysis, new projects, and community support.
- **Website:** BitcoinTalk
- **Stack Exchange:**
  - **Overview:** Stack Exchange offers a crypto-specific Q&A site for technical questions and community support. It is a valuable resource for developers and users seeking detailed answers to complex cryptocurrency-related queries.
  - **Website:** Crypto Stack Exchange

Educational Platforms:

- **Investopedia:**
  - **Overview:** Investopedia provides articles and tutorials on cryptocurrency basics and advanced topics. It is a trusted source for financial education and offers detailed explanations of various crypto concepts.
  - **Content:** The platform features guides, how-to articles, and educational videos covering a wide range of cryptocurrency topics.
  - **Website:** Investopedia
- **Coursera:**
  - **Overview:** Coursera offers online courses on blockchain and cryptocurrencies from leading universities and institutions. These courses cover fundamental concepts as well as advanced topics.
  - **Content:** Popular courses include "Bitcoin and Cryptocurrency Technologies" from Princeton University and "Blockchain Basics" from the University at Buffalo.
  - **Website:** Coursera
- **CryptoZombies:**
  - **Overview:** CryptoZombies provides interactive coding tutorials to learn Ethereum blockchain development. It is an excellent resource for those

interested in learning how to develop smart contracts and DApps.
- **Content:** The platform offers step-by-step lessons that guide users through writing and deploying smart contracts on the Ethereum blockchain.
- **Website:** CryptoZombies

Chapter 6 of "Crypto for Beginners: A Step-by-Step Guide to Digital Currency Investing" provides comprehensive guidance on staying informed and safe in the dynamic world of cryptocurrency. This section details reliable news sources, market data platforms, community forums, and educational resources to ensure beginners have access to the latest information and can make well-informed investment decisions.

Section 2: Security Best Practices

2.1 Protecting Your Investments from Scams and Hacks

Secure Wallets:

- **Hardware Wallets:**
  - **Devices like Ledger Nano S and Trezor:**
    - **Overview:** Hardware wallets are physical devices designed to securely store private keys offline, making them immune to online hacking attempts. They are considered one of the safest ways to store cryptocurrencies.
    - **Features:** Both Ledger Nano S and Trezor offer PIN protection, passphrase support, and backup options via recovery seed phrases. These devices connect to your computer via USB and require confirmation of transactions on the device itself, adding an extra layer of security.

- ▪ **Usage:** To use a hardware wallet, you need to connect it to a computer or mobile device, enter the PIN, and confirm transactions physically on the device.
- **Software Wallets:**
    - ○ **Secure Apps like Exodus and Electrum:**
        - ▪ **Overview:** Software wallets are applications that store private keys on your device. They offer greater convenience and ease of access compared to hardware wallets.
        - ▪ **Security Features:** Secure software wallets like Exodus and Electrum use encryption to protect private keys and offer backup options such as recovery phrases. They also provide integration with hardware wallets for enhanced security.
        - ▪ **Usage:** Download the wallet application from the official website or app store, set up an account, and ensure that encryption and backup options are enabled .

Regular Backups:

- **Seed Phrases:**
    - ○ **Safely Storing Your Wallet's Seed Phrase:**
        - ▪ **Overview:** A seed phrase is a series of words generated by your wallet that can be used to recover your wallet and funds. It is crucial to store this phrase securely.
        - ▪ **Best Practices:** Write down the seed phrase on paper and store it in multiple secure locations, such as a safe or safety deposit box. Avoid storing it digitally to protect against hacking and malware .
- **Encrypted Backups:**
    - ○ **Using Encryption to Secure Digital Backups:**
        - ▪ **Overview:** If you choose to keep digital backups of your wallet information, ensure

they are encrypted to prevent unauthorized access.
- **Tools:** Use encryption software like VeraCrypt or BitLocker to secure your digital backups. Store these encrypted files on external drives or cloud storage with strong security measures.

Phishing Prevention:

- **Email Vigilance:**
    - **Being Cautious of Phishing Emails and Links:**
        - **Overview:** Phishing attacks often involve emails that appear to be from legitimate sources, asking you to click on a link or provide sensitive information.
        - **Best Practices:** Always verify the sender's email address, avoid clicking on suspicious links, and never provide sensitive information through email. Use email security features to filter potential phishing attempts.
- **Secure Browsing:**
    - **Using Secure Browsers and Enabling Phishing Protection Features:**
        - **Overview:** Secure browsers like Firefox and Chrome offer built-in phishing protection features that can help prevent phishing attacks.
        - **Best Practices:** Enable phishing and malware protection in your browser settings, use browser extensions like HTTPS Everywhere and Privacy Badger, and ensure your browser is always updated to the latest version.

2.2 Importance of Two-Factor Authentication and Regular Updates

Two-Factor Authentication (2FA):

- **Setup:**
    - **Enabling 2FA on All Cryptocurrency Exchanges and Wallet Accounts:**
        - **Overview:** Two-factor authentication adds an extra layer of security by requiring a second form of verification, such as a code from an authenticator app, in addition to your password.
        - **Best Practices:** Enable 2FA on all accounts related to your cryptocurrency holdings, including exchanges and wallets. Use reputable 2FA methods to enhance security.
- **Methods:**
    - **Using Apps like Google Authenticator or Hardware Keys like YubiKey:**
        - **Google Authenticator:** A widely used app that generates time-based one-time passwords (TOTPs) for 2FA. It is free and easy to set up.
        - **YubiKey:** A hardware-based 2FA method that offers high security by requiring physical presence to authenticate. YubiKey supports multiple protocols, including OTP and FIDO2.
        - **Usage:** Download and set up the Google Authenticator app or configure your YubiKey with supported platforms for enhanced security.

Regular Updates:

- **Wallet Software:**
    - **Keeping Wallet Apps and Firmware Up to Date to Protect Against Vulnerabilities:**
        - **Overview:** Regular updates to wallet software and firmware patch known vulnerabilities and enhance security features.

- **Best Practices:** Always use the latest version of your wallet software and firmware. Enable automatic updates if available, and periodically check for updates manually.
- Antivirus and Anti-malware:
  - **Regularly Updating Security Software to Protect Devices from Malware and Hacking Attempts:**
    - **Overview:** Keeping your antivirus and anti-malware software updated is crucial for protecting your devices against new and evolving threats.
    - **Best Practices:** Use reputable security software, enable automatic updates, and run regular scans to detect and remove potential threats. Consider using additional security measures like firewalls and VPNs for enhanced protection.

Chapter 6 of "Crypto for Beginners: A Step-by-Step Guide to Digital Currency Investing" provides comprehensive guidance on staying informed and safe in the dynamic world of cryptocurrency. This section details essential security best practices, including using secure wallets, protecting against scams and hacks, enabling two-factor authentication, and keeping your software updated. By following these guidelines, beginners can safeguard their investments and navigate the cryptocurrency market with confidence.

Section 3: Recognizing and Avoiding Scams

3.1 Common Cryptocurrency Scams and How to Spot Them

Ponzi Schemes:

- **Characteristics:**
  - **Promises of High Returns with Little Risk:** Ponzi schemes entice investors by promising exceptionally high returns with little to no risk. These schemes rely on the influx of new investors' funds to pay returns to earlier investors, creating a facade of profitability.
  - **Reliance on New Investors:** The scheme collapses when the flow of new investments slows down, as there is no actual profit being generated.
- **Examples:**
  - **BitConnect:** A notorious Ponzi scheme that promised massive returns through a trading bot, which later turned out to be fraudulent. Investors were paid returns from the funds of new investors until the scheme collapsed in January 2018, leading to significant financial losses for many.

Phishing Scams:

- **Email and Website Phishing:**
  - **Recognizing Fake Emails and Websites:** Phishing scams often involve emails that appear to come from legitimate cryptocurrency exchanges or wallets, prompting users to click on links or download attachments that lead to fake websites designed to steal login credentials.
  - **Indicators:** Look for discrepancies in email addresses, grammatical errors, and urgency in the message. Always verify the sender and avoid clicking on suspicious links.
- **Social Media Scams:**
  - **Avoiding Scams on Platforms Like Twitter and Facebook:** Scammers often create fake profiles that mimic well-known figures in the cryptocurrency space, promising giveaways or investments. They typically ask users to send a small amount of cryptocurrency to receive a larger amount in return.
  - **Indicators:** Genuine giveaways do not require participants to send money first. Always verify the

legitimacy of profiles and offers through official channels.

Investment Scams:

- **Fake ICOs:**
    - **Distinguishing Legitimate ICOs from Fraudulent Ones:** Initial Coin Offerings (ICOs) are a popular method for new projects to raise funds. However, some fraudulent ICOs are created solely to steal investors' money.
    - **Research:** Always research the project's whitepaper, team members, and roadmap. Verify the credibility of the team through professional networks like LinkedIn and look for endorsements from reputable figures in the industry.
- **Pump and Dump Schemes:**
    - **Recognizing Coordinated Efforts to Inflate a Cryptocurrency's Price:** These schemes involve artificially inflating the price of a cryptocurrency through coordinated buying, often in private groups or social media channels, followed by selling off the assets at the peak, leaving other investors with significant losses.
    - **Indicators:** Be wary of sudden, unexplained spikes in a cryptocurrency's price and avoid investing based on hype from unverified sources.

3.2 Steps to Take if You Suspect Fraudulent Activity

Immediate Actions:

- **Reporting:**
    - **Reporting the Scam to Relevant Authorities and Platforms:** If you suspect you have been targeted by a scam, report it to the relevant authorities, such as the SEC or CFTC in the US, and the platform where

the scam occurred. Many cryptocurrency exchanges have procedures for reporting fraudulent activities.
- **Cease Transactions:**
  - **Stopping Any Further Transactions with Suspected Fraudulent Entities:** Immediately cease all transactions with the entity in question and withdraw any remaining funds to a secure wallet.

Recovering Funds:

- **Chargebacks:**
  - **Contacting Banks or Credit Card Companies for Chargebacks:** If you used a bank or credit card for the transaction, contact your bank or card issuer to request a chargeback. Explain the situation and provide any necessary documentation.
- **Legal Recourse:**
  - **Consulting with Legal Professionals for Potential Recovery Options:** In some cases, legal action may be necessary to recover lost funds. Consult with a lawyer who specializes in financial fraud and cryptocurrency to explore your options.

Enhanced Security Measures:

- **Account Monitoring:**
  - **Regularly Monitoring Accounts for Unusual Activity:** Keep a close eye on all cryptocurrency accounts and wallets for any signs of unauthorized activity. Set up alerts for transactions to stay informed of any changes.
- **Security Audits:**
  - **Periodically Conducting Security Audits of Your Digital Assets and Practices:** Regularly review your security practices and perform audits of your digital assets to identify and address potential vulnerabilities.

Chapter 6 of "Crypto for Beginners: A Step-by-Step Guide to Digital Currency Investing" offers detailed guidance on staying informed about cryptocurrency developments, implementing best security practices, and recognizing and avoiding common scams. By understanding the various types of scams and knowing how to protect yourself, you can ensure a safe and secure investing experience in the cryptocurrency market.

Chapter 7: Crypto ETFs: A New Frontier

Section 1: Introduction to Crypto ETFs

1.1 What Are Crypto ETFs and How They Work

Definition:

- **Crypto ETFs (Exchange-Traded Funds):**
    - Crypto ETFs are investment funds that track the performance of a specific cryptocurrency or a basket of cryptocurrencies. These funds are traded on traditional stock exchanges, providing a bridge between conventional finance and the cryptocurrency market.
    - Crypto ETFs allow investors to gain exposure to the price movements of cryptocurrencies without directly owning the underlying assets. This makes them a popular choice for those who want to invest in the cryptocurrency market without dealing with the complexities of managing digital wallets and private keys.

Mechanism:

- **Trading Like Regular Stocks:**

- - Crypto ETFs can be bought and sold on traditional stock exchanges, similar to how stocks and other ETFs are traded. This means that investors can trade them during regular market hours using standard brokerage accounts.
  - **Tracking Price Movements:**
  - These funds track the price movements of the underlying assets through various methods. Some crypto ETFs hold the actual cryptocurrencies in their portfolios, while others use derivative contracts like futures and options to replicate the performance of the cryptocurrencies they track.

1.2 Benefits of Investing in Crypto ETFs

Diversification:

- **Exposure to Multiple Cryptocurrencies:**
  - Crypto ETFs provide exposure to a diversified portfolio of cryptocurrencies. This helps reduce the risk associated with investing in a single cryptocurrency by spreading the investment across multiple digital assets.
  - **Example:** A crypto ETF might include a mix of Bitcoin, Ethereum, Litecoin, and other major cryptocurrencies, allowing investors to benefit from the overall growth of the cryptocurrency market rather than the performance of a single asset.

Accessibility:

- **For Traditional Investors:**
  - Crypto ETFs make it easier for traditional investors to enter the cryptocurrency market. Since these ETFs are traded on conventional stock exchanges, investors can use their existing brokerage accounts to buy and sell them without needing to set up cryptocurrency wallets or navigate unfamiliar platforms.

- **Example:** An investor who is familiar with trading stocks and mutual funds can seamlessly add crypto ETFs to their portfolio, benefiting from cryptocurrency exposure without needing specialized knowledge or tools.

Security:

- **Reduced Need to Manage Private Keys and Digital Wallets:**
  - One of the significant advantages of crypto ETFs is that they eliminate the need for investors to manage private keys and digital wallets. This reduces the risk of losing funds due to forgotten passwords, misplaced private keys, or hacking incidents.
  - **Example:** By investing in a crypto ETF, investors can avoid the complexities and security risks associated with directly holding cryptocurrencies, such as securing a hardware wallet or navigating the intricacies of blockchain transactions.

Professional Management:

- **Managed by Experienced Professionals:**
  - Crypto ETFs are typically managed by experienced financial professionals who continuously monitor and adjust the fund's holdings to optimize performance and manage risk. This professional management ensures that the ETF remains well-balanced and aligned with its investment objectives.
  - **Example:** Fund managers may rebalance the ETF's portfolio to maintain the desired allocation of cryptocurrencies or to adjust to changing market conditions, ensuring that the fund stays on track to meet its investment goals.

Chapter 7 of "Crypto for Beginners: A Step-by-Step Guide to Digital Currency Investing" introduces readers to the concept of Crypto ETFs, explaining how they work and their benefits. This section provides a comprehensive overview, highlighting how Crypto ETFs offer diversification, accessibility, security, and professional management, making them an attractive option for both traditional and new investors looking to enter the cryptocurrency market.

Section 2: Types of Crypto ETFs

2.1 Physically-Backed ETFs

Definition:

- **Physically-Backed ETFs:**
    - These are ETFs that hold the actual cryptocurrency in reserve. The value of the ETF is directly tied to the price of the underlying cryptocurrency it holds. When you invest in a physically-backed ETF, you are indirectly investing in the cryptocurrency itself because the fund holds the digital asset in cold storage.

Examples:

- **Fidelity Bitcoin ETF:**
    - The Fidelity Bitcoin ETF is an example of a physically-backed ETF. It directly holds Bitcoin, which means its value fluctuates in direct correlation with the price of Bitcoin. Fidelity, a well-known financial services company, manages this ETF, ensuring that the Bitcoin is securely stored and regularly audited to confirm the holdings.

2.2 Futures-Based ETFs

Definition:

- **Futures-Based ETFs:**
    - These ETFs track the price of cryptocurrency futures rather than holding the cryptocurrency itself. Futures are financial contracts obligating the buyer to purchase, and the seller to sell, an asset at a predetermined future date and price. Futures-based ETFs are typically used to gain exposure to the price movements of cryptocurrencies without holding the actual digital assets.

Examples:

- **ProShares Bitcoin Strategy ETF:**
    - The ProShares Bitcoin Strategy ETF is a prominent example of a futures-based ETF. It tracks Bitcoin futures contracts traded on the Chicago Mercantile Exchange (CME). This ETF allows investors to speculate on the future price of Bitcoin without needing to own or manage the cryptocurrency directly.

2.3 Equity-Based ETFs

Definition:

- **Equity-Based ETFs:**
    - These ETFs invest in stocks of companies involved in the blockchain and cryptocurrency industry. Instead of holding cryptocurrencies or futures contracts, equity-based ETFs hold shares of companies that are expected to benefit from the growth and adoption of blockchain technology and digital assets.

Examples:

- **Global Blockchain ETF:**
    - The Global Blockchain ETF is an example of an equity-based ETF. It includes companies like Nvidia, which produces graphics processing units (GPUs)

used in cryptocurrency mining, and IBM, which is heavily involved in blockchain technology development. This ETF offers exposure to the broader blockchain and cryptocurrency ecosystem by investing in a diversified portfolio of related companies.

Chapter 7 of "Crypto for Beginners: A Step-by-Step Guide to Digital Currency Investing" provides a comprehensive overview of Crypto ETFs, explaining their various types and benefits. This section delves into physically-backed ETFs, futures-based ETFs, and equity-based ETFs, providing real-world examples to help readers understand the nuances of each investment vehicle. By exploring these options, beginners can make informed decisions about incorporating Crypto ETFs into their investment portfolios.

Section 3: Popular Crypto ETFs

3.1 Overview of Leading ETFs

ProShares Bitcoin Strategy ETF (BITO):

- **Focuses on Bitcoin Futures Contracts:**
    o The ProShares Bitcoin Strategy ETF is designed to provide investors with exposure to Bitcoin by investing in Bitcoin futures contracts rather than directly holding the cryptocurrency. This approach allows the ETF to track the price movements of Bitcoin while using a regulated futures market.
- **Launched in October 2021:**
    o BITO made headlines as the first U.S. Bitcoin-linked ETF to be approved by the Securities and Exchange Commission (SEC). Its launch marked a significant milestone for the cryptocurrency industry, providing

traditional investors with a new way to gain exposure to Bitcoin without needing to buy and store the digital asset themselves.

Grayscale Bitcoin Trust (GBTC):

- **One of the Largest and Most Popular Bitcoin Investment Products:**
  - Grayscale Bitcoin Trust (GBTC) is a widely recognized investment vehicle that allows investors to gain exposure to Bitcoin through a trust that holds actual Bitcoin in its reserves. It operates similarly to an ETF but is structured as a trust, making it available to institutional and accredited investors.
- **Holds Actual Bitcoin in Its Reserves:**
  - GBTC's value is directly tied to the price of Bitcoin, as the trust holds Bitcoin on behalf of its investors. This makes it a popular choice for those looking to invest in Bitcoin through a traditional financial product without managing the complexities of direct cryptocurrency ownership.

Bitwise Crypto Industry Innovators ETF (BITQ):

- **Invests in Companies Involved in the Crypto and Blockchain Sectors:**
  - The Bitwise Crypto Industry Innovators ETF (BITQ) is designed to provide exposure to companies that derive significant revenue from the cryptocurrency and blockchain sectors. This includes firms involved in crypto mining, trading, and infrastructure development.
- **Focus on Innovation:**
  - BITQ includes companies like Coinbase, MicroStrategy, and other key players in the crypto industry. By investing in these companies, the ETF offers a diversified way to gain exposure to the broader cryptocurrency ecosystem and its growth potential.

Fidelity Crypto Industry and Digital Payments ETF (FDIG):

- **Focuses on Cryptocurrency, Blockchain, and Digital Payments:**
    - The Fidelity Crypto Industry and Digital Payments ETF (FDIG) aims to provide exposure to companies that are involved in the development and implementation of cryptocurrency, blockchain technology, and digital payment systems.
- **Involvement in Emerging Technologies:**
    - FDIG invests in firms that are at the forefront of digital payments and blockchain innovation, such as PayPal, Square, and other financial technology companies. This ETF offers investors a way to participate in the growth of digital payments and blockchain technologies through a diversified investment vehicle.

Chapter 7 of "Crypto for Beginners: A Step-by-Step Guide to Digital Currency Investing" provides a comprehensive overview of popular Crypto ETFs. This section details leading ETFs like the ProShares Bitcoin Strategy ETF, Grayscale Bitcoin Trust, Bitwise Crypto Industry Innovators ETF, and Fidelity Crypto Industry and Digital Payments ETF. By understanding these options, beginners can make informed decisions about incorporating Crypto ETFs into their investment portfolios.

Section 4: How to Invest in Crypto ETFs

4.1 Steps to Buying Crypto ETFs Through Traditional Brokerage Accounts

Choosing a Brokerage:

- **Selecting a Brokerage That Offers Access to Crypto ETFs:**

- When looking to invest in Crypto ETFs, the first step is to choose a brokerage that provides access to these investment vehicles. Some of the well-known brokerages offering Crypto ETFs include Fidelity, Charles Schwab, and Robinhood.
- **Considerations:**
    - **Fees:** Compare the fee structures of different brokerages. Some may offer commission-free trading, while others might have lower expense ratios for their ETF offerings.
    - **Platform Usability:** Ensure the platform is user-friendly and meets your trading needs, including features like research tools and customer support.
    - **Security:** Verify the brokerage's security measures to protect your investments and personal information.

Account Setup:

- **Opening and Funding a Brokerage Account:**
    - **Opening an Account:** Once you've selected a brokerage, the next step is to open an account. This typically involves providing personal information, such as your name, address, Social Security number, and employment details.
    - **Funding the Account:** After your account is set up, you need to fund it by transferring money from your bank account. Most brokerages offer multiple funding options, including wire transfers, ACH transfers, and even checks.

Placing an Order:

- **Searching for the Ticker Symbol of the Desired ETF:**
    - Use the brokerage's search function to find the specific Crypto ETF you wish to invest in. Each ETF has a unique ticker symbol, such as BITO for the ProShares Bitcoin Strategy ETF.

- **Placing a Buy Order:**
    - **Order Type:** Decide on the type of order you want to place. Common order types include market orders (buying at the current market price) and limit orders (buying only at a specified price or better).
    - **Number of Shares:** Specify the number of shares you want to purchase.
    - **Execution:** Review and confirm your order details before executing the trade. Once placed, your order will be processed, and the ETF shares will be added to your portfolio.

4.2 Understanding Fees and Management Costs

Management Fees:

- **Annual Fees Charged by the ETF Provider:**
    - Management fees are the costs associated with the administration and operation of the ETF. These fees are typically expressed as an annual percentage of the fund's assets and are deducted from the fund's returns.
    - **Example:** If an ETF has a management fee of 0.75%, you will pay $7.50 annually for every $1,000 invested. This fee covers the costs of managing the fund, including portfolio management, administrative expenses, and other operational costs.

Trading Fees:

- **Brokerage Fees for Buying and Selling ETF Shares:**
    - When buying or selling Crypto ETFs, you may incur trading fees charged by your brokerage. These fees can vary widely between brokerages, with some offering commission-free trades and others charging a flat fee per trade.

- **Example:** A brokerage might charge a $4.95 fee for each trade, meaning you'll pay this amount when you buy and again when you sell shares of the ETF.

Expense Ratios:

- **The Total Annual Cost Expressed as a Percentage of the Fund's Assets:**
  - The expense ratio represents the total annual cost of managing the ETF, including management fees and other operational expenses. It is expressed as a percentage of the fund's average assets under management (AUM).
  - **Example:** An ETF with an expense ratio of 1% will cost you $10 annually for every $1,000 invested. Lower expense ratios are generally preferred as they reduce the drag on investment returns.

Chapter 7 of "Crypto for Beginners: A Step-by-Step Guide to Digital Currency Investing" provides a comprehensive guide on how to invest in Crypto ETFs. This section details the steps to buying Crypto ETFs through traditional brokerage accounts, including choosing a brokerage, setting up an account, and placing an order. It also explains the importance of understanding fees and management costs, ensuring beginners are well-informed about the financial aspects of investing in Crypto ETFs.

Section 5: Risks and Considerations

5.1 Volatility and Tracking Errors

Volatility:

- **Crypto ETFs are Subject to the Same Volatility as the Underlying Cryptocurrencies:**
    - Cryptocurrencies are known for their extreme price volatility, often experiencing significant price swings within short periods. This inherent volatility is reflected in crypto ETFs as well. When the price of the underlying cryptocurrency experiences a sharp rise or fall, the value of the corresponding ETF will mirror these movements.
    - **Example:** The price of Bitcoin, which serves as the underlying asset for many crypto ETFs, has experienced significant fluctuations. For instance, Bitcoin's price surged from around $10,000 in early 2020 to over $60,000 in April 2021, only to drop below $30,000 by July 2021. Such volatility directly impacts the performance of Bitcoin-linked ETFs like the ProShares Bitcoin Strategy ETF (BITO).
- **Price Swings Can Be Significant and Frequent:**
    - Investors in crypto ETFs need to be prepared for frequent and sometimes drastic price changes. This volatility can present opportunities for high returns but also poses significant risks.
    - **Example:** In November 2021, the price of Bitcoin fell by over 15% in just one day, demonstrating how rapidly market conditions can change. Such movements can lead to substantial gains or losses for ETF investors within a very short timeframe.

Tracking Errors:

- **Differences Between the ETF's Performance and the Underlying Asset's Price:**
    - Tracking error refers to the difference between the performance of the ETF and the performance of its underlying assets. This discrepancy can occur due to several factors, including management fees, trading costs, and imperfect replication of the underlying asset's performance.

- **Management Fees:** ETF providers charge management fees for their services, which can slightly reduce the overall returns of the ETF compared to the direct performance of the underlying cryptocurrency.
- **Imperfect Replication:** Especially for futures-based ETFs, the fund may not perfectly track the spot price of the cryptocurrency. Futures prices can differ from the spot prices due to factors like market expectations and contract expirations.

5.2 Regulatory Risks and Market Sentiment

Regulatory Risks:

- **Changes in Regulations Can Impact the Availability and Performance of Crypto ETFs:**
    - The regulatory environment for cryptocurrencies and related financial products is continually evolving. Regulatory changes can significantly impact the performance and availability of crypto ETFs. For example, new regulations may impose restrictions on trading, increase compliance costs, or even lead to the delisting of certain ETFs.
    - **Example:** In September 2021, China announced a comprehensive ban on all cryptocurrency transactions and mining, which caused a significant market sell-off and impacted crypto ETF prices globally.
- **Ongoing Regulatory Scrutiny and Potential for New Rules:**
    - Crypto ETFs are under constant scrutiny by regulatory bodies such as the U.S. Securities and Exchange Commission (SEC). The potential for new rules or changes in existing regulations can create uncertainty and affect investor sentiment.

- **Example:** The SEC's delay or denial of approval for various Bitcoin ETFs has historically led to market volatility and impacted investor confidence.

Market Sentiment:

- **Investor Perception and News Can Heavily Influence the Performance of Crypto ETFs:**
    - Market sentiment plays a crucial role in the performance of crypto ETFs. Positive news such as technological advancements, institutional adoption, or favorable regulatory developments can drive investor interest and inflows into crypto ETFs.
    - **Example:** When Tesla announced it had purchased $1.5 billion in Bitcoin in February 2021, the price of Bitcoin surged, positively affecting Bitcoin ETFs.
- **Negative News Can Lead to Significant Sell-Offs:**
    - Conversely, negative developments such as security breaches, regulatory crackdowns, or adverse market events can lead to significant sell-offs and negatively impact the performance of crypto ETFs.
    - **Example:** The hack of the cryptocurrency exchange Mt. Gox in 2014 resulted in a major loss of confidence and a significant drop in Bitcoin prices, highlighting how security issues can affect market sentiment and ETF performance.

Chapter 7 of "Crypto for Beginners: A Step-by-Step Guide to Digital Currency Investing" provides a comprehensive overview of Crypto ETFs, including their types, benefits, leading examples, steps for investing, and associated risks and considerations. By understanding the potential risks such as volatility, tracking errors, regulatory risks, and the influence of market sentiment, beginners can make informed decisions and better manage their investments in Crypto ETFs.

Chapter 8: Advanced Topics in Crypto Investing

Section 1: DeFi (Decentralized Finance)

1.1 Overview of DeFi and Its Potential Impact

Definition:

- **Decentralized Finance (DeFi):**
    - DeFi refers to a broad range of financial applications built on blockchain technology that aim to disrupt traditional financial intermediaries like banks and brokers. DeFi leverages the decentralized nature of blockchain to create open, transparent, and accessible financial systems.

Core Principles:

- **Decentralization:**
    - DeFi removes intermediaries from financial transactions, allowing peer-to-peer interactions. Smart contracts on blockchain networks, primarily Ethereum, enable these transactions without the need for a central authority.
    - **Example:** In a DeFi loan, instead of borrowing from a bank, you borrow directly from a peer, with the terms encoded in a smart contract that automatically enforces them.
- **Transparency:**
    - DeFi platforms operate on open-source protocols. Transactions are recorded on public blockchains, making them transparent and immutable. This transparency reduces the risk of fraud and enhances trust in the system.
    - **Example:** All transactions on platforms like Uniswap or Aave can be viewed and verified on the Ethereum blockchain explorer, Etherscan.

- **Accessibility:**
    - DeFi services are available to anyone with an internet connection, breaking down barriers imposed by traditional banking systems. This inclusivity is particularly beneficial for individuals in regions with limited access to financial services.
    - **Example:** Users in countries with underdeveloped banking infrastructure can participate in global financial markets using DeFi platforms.

Potential Impact:

- **Financial Inclusion:**
    - DeFi has the potential to provide financial services to the unbanked and underbanked populations globally. By eliminating the need for traditional banking infrastructure, DeFi can offer savings, loans, and investment opportunities to anyone with internet access.
    - **Example:** A farmer in a rural area without a local bank can access global financial services through a mobile phone and a DeFi platform.
- **Efficiency:**
    - DeFi enables faster and cheaper financial transactions by removing intermediaries and automating processes with smart contracts. This efficiency can significantly reduce transaction costs and time.
    - **Example:** International money transfers that take days and incur high fees through traditional banks can be completed in minutes with minimal fees using DeFi platforms like Stellar.
- **Innovation:**
    - DeFi fosters innovation by enabling new financial products and services that were not possible in traditional finance. These innovations include decentralized exchanges, automated market makers, yield farming, and more.
    - **Example:** Yield farming allows users to earn interest on their cryptocurrency holdings by providing

liquidity to DeFi protocols, something not feasible in the traditional financial system.

1.2 Key DeFi Platforms and How to Invest in Them

Platforms:

- **Uniswap:**
    - **Overview:** Uniswap is a decentralized exchange (DEX) that allows users to trade cryptocurrencies directly from their wallets without the need for an intermediary. It uses an automated market maker (AMM) system to facilitate trading.
    - **How It Works:** Users provide liquidity to pools and earn fees from trades made in those pools. This system ensures continuous liquidity and decentralized trading.
- **Aave:**
    - **Overview:** Aave is a decentralized lending platform where users can borrow and lend cryptocurrencies. It offers a range of features, including flash loans, which are instant loans that must be repaid within the same transaction.
    - **How It Works:** Users can deposit cryptocurrencies into Aave's liquidity pools and earn interest. Borrowers can take out loans against their deposited assets as collateral.
- **Compound:**
    - **Overview:** Compound is an algorithmic, autonomous interest rate protocol that allows users to lend and borrow cryptocurrencies. Interest rates are set algorithmically based on supply and demand.
    - **How It Works:** Users can supply assets to liquidity pools and earn interest or borrow assets against their collateral. Interest accrues in real-time and is automatically compounded.
- **MakerDAO:**
    - **Overview:** MakerDAO is a decentralized credit platform that supports the Dai stablecoin, which is

pegged to the US dollar. It allows users to generate Dai by depositing collateral in the form of Ether (ETH) or other accepted cryptocurrencies.
    - **How It Works:** Users lock up collateral in smart contracts and generate Dai based on the collateral's value. The system includes mechanisms to ensure the stable value of Dai.

How to Invest:

- **Research:**
    - Before investing in any DeFi platform, it is crucial to understand the fundamentals of the platform, including its technology, team, and security measures. Look for credible sources of information and reviews from the community.
    - **Example:** Check the platform's whitepaper, audit reports, and community discussions on forums like Reddit or GitHub.
- **Participation:**
    - **Lending and Borrowing:** Use DeFi platforms to lend or borrow cryptocurrencies. For example, deposit assets into Aave to earn interest or take out a loan against your crypto holdings.
    - **Providing Liquidity:** Provide liquidity to DEXs like Uniswap and earn a share of the trading fees. This involves depositing pairs of tokens into liquidity pools.
- **Governance Tokens:**
    - Many DeFi platforms issue governance tokens that give holders voting rights on protocol changes and decisions. These tokens can also appreciate in value.
    - **Examples:** UNI (Uniswap), AAVE (Aave), and COMP (Compound). Investing in these tokens provides a stake in the platform's future and potential profits from their appreciation.

Chapter 8 of "Crypto for Beginners: A Step-by-Step Guide to Digital Currency Investing" delves into advanced topics, starting with an overview of Decentralized Finance (DeFi). This section explains the core principles and potential impact of DeFi, introduces key platforms, and provides guidance on how to invest in them. By understanding DeFi, beginners can explore new opportunities in the evolving cryptocurrency landscape and make informed investment decisions.

Section 2: NFTs (Non-Fungible Tokens)

2.1 What Are NFTs and How They Work

Definition:

- **Non-Fungible Tokens (NFTs):**
  - NFTs are unique digital assets that represent ownership of a specific item or piece of content, verified using blockchain technology. Unlike cryptocurrencies such as Bitcoin or Ethereum, which are fungible and can be exchanged on a one-to-one basis, NFTs are distinct and cannot be exchanged on a like-for-like basis.

How They Work:

- **Uniqueness:**
  - Each NFT contains distinct information that differentiates it from other NFTs. This metadata, stored on the blockchain, includes details such as the creator, ownership history, and unique attributes of the asset, making each NFT one-of-a-kind.
  - **Example:** The NFT for a digital artwork will include data about the artist, the creation date, and any subsequent sales or transfers.
- **Blockchain Verification:**

- The ownership and transaction history of NFTs are recorded on a blockchain, providing a secure and transparent way to verify authenticity and provenance. This ensures that the digital asset is genuine and can be traced back to its origin.
- **Example:** Ethereum is the most commonly used blockchain for NFTs, utilizing the ERC-721 and ERC-1155 token standards to create and manage NFTs.

Use Cases:

- **Digital Art:**
    - Artists are increasingly selling their digital art as NFTs, providing a new revenue stream and greater control over their work. Notable examples include Beeple's "Everydays: The First 5000 Days," which sold for $69 million at a Christie's auction.
    - **Example:** Digital artists can embed royalties into their NFTs, ensuring they receive a percentage of sales each time the artwork is resold on secondary markets.
- **Collectibles:**
    - NFTs are popular in the digital collectibles space, allowing users to buy, sell, and trade unique digital items. Projects like CryptoKitties and NBA Top Shot have gained significant attention.
    - **Example:** CryptoKitties allows users to breed and trade virtual cats, each with unique attributes, while NBA Top Shot offers collectible highlights of NBA games.
- **Virtual Real Estate:**
    - NFTs are also used to buy and sell virtual land in online platforms like Decentraland and The Sandbox. Users can purchase, develop, and trade parcels of virtual real estate.
    - **Example:** In Decentraland, users can create and monetize experiences on their virtual land, such as virtual galleries, games, and social hubs.

2.2 Investing in NFTs: Opportunities and Risks

Opportunities:

- **Ownership of Unique Assets:**
    - NFTs provide the opportunity to own unique digital items, ranging from art and music to virtual real estate and collectibles. This ownership is verifiable and secure thanks to blockchain technology.
    - **Example:** Collectors can own exclusive digital artworks or rare virtual items that have intrinsic and market value.
- **Supporting Artists:**
    - NFTs allow collectors to directly support creators and artists by purchasing their work. This decentralized model can empower artists by providing them with new revenue streams and greater control over their creations.
    - **Example:** Artists can receive royalties from secondary sales, ensuring ongoing revenue each time their work changes hands.
- **Potential for High Returns:**
    - Some NFTs have appreciated significantly in value, offering substantial returns to early investors. High-profile sales and increasing mainstream adoption have driven demand for certain NFTs.
    - **Example:** Early investors in CryptoPunks, a series of unique 24x24 pixel art images, have seen their investments skyrocket as the project gained popularity.

Risks:

- **Market Volatility:**
    - The NFT market can be highly volatile, with prices subject to significant fluctuations based on market trends, investor sentiment, and speculation.

- **Example:** An NFT that sells for thousands of dollars today could significantly drop in value if market interest wanes or if the project loses popularity.
- **Liquidity Issues:**
    - Unlike fungible tokens, NFTs can be harder to sell quickly due to their unique nature. Finding a buyer willing to pay the desired price for a specific NFT can take time.
    - **Example:** Selling a unique digital artwork may require finding a niche collector interested in that particular piece, which can delay transactions and impact liquidity.
- **Speculation and Hype:**
    - The NFT market is often driven by speculation and hype, leading to inflated prices and potential bubbles. Investors need to be cautious and conduct thorough research before making purchases.
    - **Example:** The rapid rise and fall of certain NFT projects, driven by social media hype and speculative buying, can result in significant losses for investors who buy at peak prices.

Chapter 8 of "Crypto for Beginners: A Step-by-Step Guide to Digital Currency Investing" delves into advanced topics, including the burgeoning field of Non-Fungible Tokens (NFTs). This section provides a comprehensive explanation of what NFTs are, how they work, and their various use cases. It also explores the opportunities and risks associated with investing in NFTs, offering real-world examples and insights to help beginners navigate this exciting and rapidly evolving market.

Section 3: Staking and Yield Farming

3.1 How to Earn Passive Income with Cryptocurrencies

Staking:

- **Definition:**
  - Staking involves locking up a portion of cryptocurrency to support the operations of a blockchain network. In return, participants earn rewards, usually in the form of additional cryptocurrency. Staking is integral to Proof-of-Stake (PoS) and its variants, where validators are chosen to create new blocks and confirm transactions based on the number of coins they hold and are willing to "stake" as collateral.
- **How It Works:**
  - Participants lock their coins in a staking wallet, which involves delegating their stake to a validator who performs network operations on their behalf. In return, stakers receive rewards, often calculated based on the number of coins staked and the duration of staking.
  - **Example:** Staking Ethereum 2.0 involves locking ETH in the Ethereum 2.0 deposit contract to help secure the network and earn rewards. Similarly, Cardano (ADA) and Polkadot (DOT) offer staking opportunities, where participants can earn rewards by contributing to network security and functionality.

Yield Farming:

- **Definition:**
  - Yield farming, also known as liquidity mining, involves earning interest by providing liquidity to DeFi (Decentralized Finance) protocols. Users lend their cryptocurrency to a protocol and, in return, earn interest, often in the form of the protocol's native tokens.
- **How It Works:**
  - Users provide liquidity by depositing their cryptocurrency into a liquidity pool on a DeFi platform. These pools facilitate trading and other functions on the platform. In return, users earn a

portion of the transaction fees and interest generated by the pool.
- **Example:** Providing liquidity on platforms like Uniswap, SushiSwap, or PancakeSwap involves depositing pairs of tokens into liquidity pools. Users earn rewards based on their share of the pool and the platform's specific reward mechanisms.

3.2 Platforms and Strategies for Staking and Yield Farming

Staking Platforms:

- **Exchanges:**
    - Centralized exchanges like Binance, Coinbase, and Kraken offer staking services. These platforms make staking accessible to users by handling the technical aspects and providing a user-friendly interface.
    - **Example:** Binance offers staking for a variety of cryptocurrencies, including Ethereum 2.0, Cardano, and Polkadot, allowing users to earn staking rewards without needing to set up their own staking infrastructure.
- **Wallets:**
    - Some wallets, like Trust Wallet and Ledger, support staking directly from the wallet. These wallets allow users to stake their assets securely while retaining control over their private keys.
    - **Example:** Ledger hardware wallets support staking for several cryptocurrencies, providing security and ease of use for those looking to stake their assets directly from their wallet.

Yield Farming Strategies:

- **Platform Selection:**
    - Choosing DeFi platforms with high liquidity and a good reputation is crucial for successful yield

farming. High liquidity ensures that transactions can be processed smoothly, while a good reputation indicates reliability and security.
    - **Example:** Uniswap and SushiSwap are popular DeFi platforms known for their high liquidity and user-friendly interfaces, making them attractive options for yield farming.
- **Risk Assessment:**
    - Evaluating the risks associated with smart contract bugs, platform security, and market volatility is essential. Smart contract vulnerabilities can lead to significant losses, so it's important to choose well-audited platforms.
    - **Example:** Before committing funds to a yield farming strategy, users should review the platform's audit reports and track record to ensure it has a robust security framework.
- **Diversification:**
    - Spreading investments across multiple platforms and liquidity pools can help minimize risk. Diversification reduces the impact of a single platform's failure or a significant market downturn on the overall investment.
    - **Example:** A yield farmer might allocate funds across several DeFi platforms like Uniswap, Compound, and Aave to balance risk and reward, ensuring that not all assets are exposed to the same risks.

Chapter 8 of "Crypto for Beginners: A Step-by-Step Guide to Digital Currency Investing" provides a detailed exploration of advanced topics such as DeFi, NFTs, and passive income strategies through staking and yield farming. This section equips readers with the knowledge to navigate and invest in these emerging areas of the cryptocurrency market, offering real-world examples and insights to help beginners make informed decisions.

Conclusion: The Future of Cryptocurrencies

Section 1: The Future of Cryptocurrencies

1.1 Potential Developments and Trends in the Crypto World

Mainstream Adoption:

- **Increasing Use of Cryptocurrencies for Everyday Transactions:**
    - Cryptocurrencies are gradually being adopted for daily transactions, from buying coffee to paying for services. Companies like PayPal, Visa, and Mastercard have integrated crypto payments, allowing consumers to use digital assets in their everyday spending. El Salvador's adoption of Bitcoin as legal tender is a significant milestone, setting a precedent for other nations to follow.
- **Major Companies and Financial Institutions Integrating Blockchain Technology:**
    - Leading corporations, including Tesla and Square, have added Bitcoin to their balance sheets, indicating a growing acceptance of cryptocurrencies as a legitimate asset class. Financial institutions such as JPMorgan and Goldman Sachs are offering crypto investment products to their clients, further legitimizing the market.

Technological Advancements:

- **Continued Development of Blockchain Scalability Solutions:**
    - Scalability remains a critical challenge for blockchain networks. Solutions such as Layer 2 scaling (e.g., Lightning Network for Bitcoin) and sharding (e.g.,

Ethereum 2.0) are being developed to enhance transaction speeds and reduce fees. These advancements are crucial for supporting the growing number of users and transactions on blockchain networks.

- **Innovations in Interoperability Between Different Blockchain Networks:**
    - Interoperability protocols, such as Polkadot and Cosmos, aim to facilitate seamless communication and transactions between different blockchain networks. This innovation is essential for creating a more interconnected and efficient blockchain ecosystem, enabling diverse applications and use cases to interact effectively.

Regulatory Evolution:

- **Governments and Regulatory Bodies Developing Clearer Frameworks:**
    - Regulatory clarity is vital for the growth and stability of the cryptocurrency market. Governments and regulatory bodies worldwide are working on establishing comprehensive frameworks to govern crypto assets. Clear regulations can reduce uncertainty, attract institutional investors, and enhance market stability.
- **Potential for Increased Legitimacy and Stability in the Market:**
    - With clearer regulations, the cryptocurrency market is likely to gain increased legitimacy. This can lead to greater adoption, reduced volatility, and enhanced investor confidence. Regulatory developments, such as the approval of Bitcoin ETFs by the U.S. SEC, are steps towards mainstream acceptance and stability.

Decentralized Finance (DeFi) Expansion:

- **Growth of DeFi Platforms:**

- DeFi platforms are revolutionizing financial services by offering decentralized lending, borrowing, and trading. The total value locked (TVL) in DeFi protocols has grown exponentially, reflecting increasing user interest and adoption. Platforms like Aave, Compound, and Uniswap are leading this transformation.
- **Enhanced Security Measures and User-Friendly Interfaces:**
    - As DeFi continues to grow, security remains a top priority. Enhanced security protocols and audits are being implemented to protect user funds. Additionally, user-friendly interfaces are being developed to make DeFi more accessible to the general public, driving wider adoption.

NFT and Digital Asset Growth:

- **Expansion of NFT Applications:**
    - While NFTs gained initial popularity through digital art and collectibles, their applications are expanding into areas like real estate and intellectual property. NFTs can represent ownership of real-world assets, making transactions more efficient and transparent.
- **Integration of NFTs into Mainstream Industries:**
    - Mainstream industries, including entertainment, sports, and fashion, are integrating NFTs into their business models. For example, major brands are using NFTs for marketing and engagement, creating unique digital experiences for their customers.

1.2 Final Thoughts and Encouragement for Beginners

Embrace the Learning Journey:

- **Cryptocurrencies and Blockchain Technology Are Still in Their Early Stages:**

- The cryptocurrency market is dynamic and rapidly evolving. As a beginner, it's essential to stay curious and continually seek to understand new developments, trends, and technologies. The potential for innovation and growth in this space is immense, and staying informed will help you navigate and capitalize on emerging opportunities.

Patience and Perseverance:

- **The Crypto Market Can Be Volatile and Unpredictable:**
  - The cryptocurrency market is known for its volatility. Prices can swing dramatically in short periods, driven by market sentiment, regulatory news, and technological advancements. As an investor, it's important to focus on long-term goals and avoid making impulsive decisions based on short-term market movements.

Community Engagement:

- **Participate in Crypto Communities and Forums:**
  - Engaging with the crypto community can provide valuable insights, support, and learning opportunities. Online forums, social media groups, and local meetups are excellent places to share knowledge, ask questions, and learn from the experiences of others.
- **Collaboration and Networking:**
  - Building connections within the crypto community can enhance your understanding and open doors to new opportunities. Networking with other enthusiasts, developers, and investors can provide a broader perspective and help you stay updated on the latest trends and innovations.

Section 2: Next Steps for New Investors

2.1 Continuous Learning and Staying Updated

Regularly Follow Reliable News Sources:

- **Stay Informed About Market Trends, Regulatory Changes, and Technological Advancements:**
    - The cryptocurrency market is dynamic and rapidly evolving. Staying informed about the latest trends, regulatory changes, and technological advancements is crucial for making informed investment decisions. Regularly following reliable news sources can help you stay ahead of the curve and adapt to market shifts.
- **Subscribe to Reputable Cryptocurrency News Platforms:**
    - Subscribing to reputable news platforms ensures you receive timely and accurate information. Some of the top platforms include:
        - **CoinDesk:** Known for its comprehensive coverage of blockchain technology, digital assets, and cryptocurrency news. It provides daily updates, in-depth articles, and expert analysis.
        - **CoinTelegraph:** Offers a wide range of articles, updates, and market analysis. It covers all aspects of the crypto industry, from price movements to regulatory news and technological advancements.
        - **CryptoSlate:** Provides news, data, and real-time information about the blockchain and cryptocurrency industry. It is known for its detailed market data and educational resources.

Participate in Webinars and Conferences:

- **Attend Industry Events, Webinars, and Conferences:**
    - Participating in industry events allows you to learn from experts and network with other investors. These events often feature panel discussions, workshops,

and presentations on the latest developments in the crypto space.
    - **Example:** Events like Consensus by CoinDesk, Blockchain Week, and DeFi Summit offer valuable insights and opportunities to connect with industry leaders.
- **Engage in Online Courses and Workshops:**
    - Online courses and workshops can deepen your understanding of specific topics, from the basics of blockchain technology to advanced trading strategies. Platforms like Coursera, Udemy, and Binance Academy offer a range of courses tailored to different skill levels.

Join Online Communities:

- **Engage with Communities on Reddit, BitcoinTalk, and Other Forums:**
    - Online communities are excellent resources for sharing knowledge, asking questions, and learning from the experiences of others. Forums like Reddit (r/Bitcoin, r/Ethereum, r/Cryptocurrency) and BitcoinTalk provide platforms for discussion and support.
- **Follow Influential Figures and Thought Leaders on Social Media:**
    - Following influential figures and thought leaders on platforms like Twitter and LinkedIn can provide valuable insights and keep you updated on the latest trends and opinions in the crypto space.
    - **Example:** Influencers like Vitalik Buterin (co-founder of Ethereum), Andreas M. Antonopoulos (Bitcoin advocate), and Meltem Demirors (Chief Strategy Officer at CoinShares) regularly share their thoughts and analyses on social media.

2.2 Building a Long-Term Investment Strategy

Set Clear Financial Goals:

- **Define Your Investment Objectives and Time Horizon:**
    - Clearly defining your investment objectives and time horizon is crucial for developing a successful investment strategy. Determine whether you are investing for short-term gains, long-term growth, or a specific financial goal.
    - **Example:** An investor might set a goal to accumulate a certain amount of cryptocurrency over five years for future financial security or retirement.
- **Establish Realistic Expectations for Returns and Risk Tolerance:**
    - Understanding your risk tolerance and setting realistic expectations for returns can help you avoid impulsive decisions and stay focused on your long-term goals. The crypto market can be highly volatile, so it's important to be prepared for significant price fluctuations.

Diversify Your Portfolio:

- **Spread Investments Across Different Cryptocurrencies, DeFi Projects, and Blockchain Companies:**
    - Diversification can help manage risk and improve the stability of your portfolio. Consider investing in a mix of major cryptocurrencies like Bitcoin and Ethereum, emerging DeFi projects, and blockchain-related companies.
    - **Example:** A diversified portfolio might include 50% in Bitcoin, 25% in Ethereum, 15% in DeFi tokens like Aave and Uniswap, and 10% in stocks of blockchain companies like Square and Nvidia.
- **Consider a Mix of Long-Term Holdings and Short-Term Trading Opportunities:**
    - Balancing long-term investments with short-term trading opportunities can provide both stability and potential for higher returns. Long-term holdings can

be more resilient to market volatility, while short-term trades can capitalize on market fluctuations.
    - **Example:** An investor might hold Bitcoin and Ethereum for the long term while actively trading smaller-cap cryptocurrencies based on market trends.

Regular Portfolio Review:

- **Periodically Review and Rebalance Your Portfolio:**
    - Regularly reviewing and rebalancing your portfolio ensures that it aligns with your goals and adapts to changing market conditions. This process involves assessing the performance of your investments and making adjustments as needed.
    - **Example:** If a particular asset has significantly appreciated, you might sell a portion to rebalance your portfolio and invest in other opportunities.
- **Stay Flexible and Adapt Your Strategy:**
    - Staying flexible and adapting your strategy based on new information and market developments is crucial for long-term success. Continuously learning and staying updated will help you make informed decisions and adjust your strategy as needed.

Adopt Best Practices for Security:

- **Use Secure Wallets and Exchanges to Protect Your Assets:**
    - Ensuring the security of your assets is paramount. Use reputable wallets and exchanges with strong security measures to protect your investments from theft and hacking.
    - **Example:** Hardware wallets like Ledger and Trezor provide secure storage for your cryptocurrencies, while exchanges like Coinbase and Kraken offer robust security features.
- **Implement Strong Passwords, Two-Factor Authentication, and Regular Backups:**

- Enhancing the security of your accounts by using strong, unique passwords, enabling two-factor authentication (2FA), and regularly backing up your wallet information can protect your investments from unauthorized access and loss.
- **Example:** Setting up 2FA on your exchange accounts and keeping multiple backups of your wallet's seed phrase in secure locations can significantly reduce security risks.

The conclusion of "Crypto for Beginners: A Step-by-Step Guide to Digital Currency Investing" provides a comprehensive wrap-up, encouraging continuous learning, strategic planning, and proactive engagement in the dynamic world of cryptocurrencies. By following these next steps, new investors can confidently navigate the evolving landscape and make informed decisions to achieve their financial goals.

Appendices

1. Glossary of Cryptocurrency Terms

1.1 Definitions of Key Terms and Jargon

- **Altcoin:**
    - Any cryptocurrency other than Bitcoin. Examples include Ethereum, Ripple, and Litecoin.
- **Blockchain:**
    - A decentralized ledger that records all transactions across a network of computers.
- **Consensus Mechanism:**

- o A protocol used by blockchain networks to agree on the validity of transactions. Examples include Proof of Work (PoW) and Proof of Stake (PoS).
- **Cryptocurrency:**
  - o A digital or virtual currency that uses cryptography for security.
- **Decentralized Finance (DeFi):**
  - o Financial services provided through decentralized blockchain networks without traditional intermediaries like banks.
- **Distributed Ledger:**
  - o A digital record of data spread across multiple locations or participants.
- **Exchange-Traded Fund (ETF):**
  - o An investment fund that tracks the performance of a particular asset or group of assets and is traded on stock exchanges.
- **Fork:**
  - o A split in the blockchain where two separate chains with the same history are created. Can be hard (permanent divergence) or soft (temporary divergence).
- **Gas:**
  - o The fee required to conduct a transaction or execute a contract on the Ethereum blockchain.
- **HODL:**
  - o A slang term in the cryptocurrency community meaning to hold onto assets rather than selling them, regardless of price volatility.
- **Initial Coin Offering (ICO):**
  - o A fundraising method where new cryptocurrencies sell a portion of their tokens to early investors.
- **Node:**
  - o A computer that participates in the blockchain network by validating and relaying transactions.
- **Non-Fungible Token (NFT):**
  - o A unique digital asset verified using blockchain technology, often used for art, collectibles, and other unique items.

- **Private Key:**
  - A secret key that allows the holder to access and manage their cryptocurrency.
- **Public Key:**
  - A key that can be shared publicly to receive cryptocurrency.
- **Smart Contract:**
  - Self-executing contracts with the terms of the agreement directly written into code on the blockchain.
- **Stablecoin:**
  - A cryptocurrency designed to have a stable value by being pegged to a reserve asset like a fiat currency or commodity.
- **Wallet:**
  - A digital tool used to store, send, and receive cryptocurrencies.

2. Useful Tools and Resources

2.1 List of Recommended Wallets

- **Hot Wallets:**
  - **Trust Wallet:** A mobile wallet supporting a wide range of cryptocurrencies.
  - **MetaMask:** A popular browser extension wallet for Ethereum and ERC-20 tokens.
  - **Coinbase Wallet:** A user-friendly wallet with built-in support for multiple assets.
- **Cold Wallets:**
  - **Ledger Nano S/X:** Hardware wallets known for their high security and support for numerous cryptocurrencies.
  - **Trezor:** Another leading hardware wallet brand offering robust security features.

2.2 List of Recommended Exchanges

- **Centralized Exchanges (CEX):**
  - **Binance:** One of the largest global cryptocurrency exchanges by trading volume.
  - **Coinbase:** A user-friendly platform ideal for beginners.
  - **Kraken:** Known for its security and wide range of supported cryptocurrencies.
- **Decentralized Exchanges (DEX):**
  - **Uniswap:** Leading DEX on the Ethereum blockchain.
  - **SushiSwap:** A DEX that started as a fork of Uniswap but has grown to offer additional features.
  - **PancakeSwap:** Popular DEX on the Binance Smart Chain.

2.3 List of Analysis Tools

- **Market Data Platforms:**
  - **CoinMarketCap:** Provides detailed information on prices, volumes, and market capitalizations of cryptocurrencies.
  - **CryptoCompare:** Offers real-time market data, charts, and portfolio tracking.
- **Technical Analysis Tools:**
  - **TradingView:** A comprehensive charting platform for analysing cryptocurrency markets.
  - **Coinigy:** A trading platform that integrates with multiple exchanges and provides advanced charting tools.

3. Frequently Asked Questions (FAQ)

3.1 Common Questions and Concise Answers for Beginners

- **What is Bitcoin?**
  - Bitcoin is the first decentralized digital currency, created by Satoshi Nakamoto. It allows peer-to-peer transactions without the need for intermediaries.

- **How do I buy cryptocurrency?**
    - You can buy cryptocurrencies through exchanges like Coinbase, Binance, or Kraken. Create an account, complete the verification process, and deposit funds to start trading.
- **What is a blockchain?**
    - A blockchain is a decentralized ledger that records all transactions across a network of computers, ensuring transparency and security.
- **How do I store my cryptocurrency safely?**
    - Use a combination of hot wallets for convenience and cold wallets for long-term storage. Enable two-factor authentication and keep your private keys secure.
- **What are gas fees?**
    - Gas fees are transaction fees paid to miners on the Ethereum network to process and validate transactions or execute smart contracts.
- **Is cryptocurrency legal?**
    - Cryptocurrency legality varies by country. It is important to understand the regulatory environment in your jurisdiction before investing.
- **What is an ICO?**
    - An Initial Coin Offering (ICO) is a fundraising method where new cryptocurrencies sell a portion of their tokens to early investors to raise capital.
- **Can I lose money in cryptocurrencies?**
    - Yes, the cryptocurrency market is highly volatile and can experience significant price swings. Only invest what you can afford to lose.
- **What is DeFi?**
    - Decentralized Finance (DeFi) refers to financial services built on blockchain technology that operate without traditional intermediaries like banks.
- **What are NFTs?**
    - Non-Fungible Tokens (NFTs) are unique digital assets that represent ownership of a specific item or piece of content, verified using blockchain technology.

This appendices for "Crypto for Beginners: A Step-by-Step Guide to Digital Currency Investing" provide comprehensive support resources, including a glossary of key terms, a list of useful tools and resources, and answers to common questions, ensuring that beginners have access to the necessary information and tools to navigate the cryptocurrency landscape effectively.

www.ingramcontent.com/pod-product-compliance
Lightning Source LLC
Chambersburg PA
CBHW070925220526
45472CB00015B/1016